The World's Greatest
Wingshooting Destinations

Chris Dorsey

Foreword by Curt Gowdy • Paintings by Penny Meakin

DEDICATION

For Amy, who shares my love of adventure and who,
even if she is a continent away, is never far from my thoughts.

The World's Greatest Wingshooting Destinations

SYCAMORE ISLAND BOOKS · BOULDER, COLORADO

Other books by Chris Dorsey:

Game Days
A Grouse Hunter's Almanac
Hunt Wisconsin

Pheasant Days
Wildfowler's Season

The World's Greatest Wingshooting Destinations by Chris Dorsey
Copyright © 2002 by Chris Dorsey

Publisher's Cataloging-in-Publication
(Provided by Quality Books, Inc.)

Dorsey, Chris, 1965–
    The world's greatest wingshooting destinations /
Chris Dorsey ; foreword by Curt Gowdy ; paintings by
Penny Meakin. -- 1st ed.
    p. cm.
    ISBN: 1-58160-294-4

    1. Fowling--Guidebooks.   I. Title.

SK313.D67 2002   799.2'4
                                  QBI02-200218

Printed in the United States of America

Published by Sycamore Island Books, a division of Paladin Enterprises, Inc.
Gunbarrel Tech Center, 7077 Winchester Circle, Boulder, Colorado 80301 USA, +1.303.443.7250.

Direct inquiries and/or orders to the above address.

All photos by Chris Dorsey unless otherwise indicated. Maps by William Tipton.

Visit our Web site at www.sycamoreisland.com

TABLE OF Contents

Foreword: Spanning the Globe by Curt Gowdy vii

Introduction: Caveat Emptor 1

PART I: EUROPE 9
REVELRY IN THE OLD WORLD

Chapter 1: Grouse of Another Time (Russia) 13

Chapter 2: A Magyar Revival (Hungary) 21

Chapter 3: Czeching Out the New Republic (Czech Republic) 29

Chapter 4: Heather or Not (Scotland) 35

Chapter 5: An Attack of Pheasants (Denmark) 43

PART II: AFRICA 49
SAFARI WINGS

Chapter 6: An African Journey (Zimbabwe) 53

Chapter 7: Africa's Feathered Treasures (South Africa) 65

Chapter 8: Flying Times in the Cape (South Africa) 75

Chapter 9: Moor and Better Wingshooting (South Africa) 85

Chapter 10: An Okavango Oasis (Botswana) 95

PART III: SOUTH AMERICA/MEXICO · · · · · · · · · · · · · · · · · · 107

AN ADDICTION OF BIRDS

Chapter 11: A Postcard from South of the Border (Mexico) · · · · · · · · · · · · · · 111
Chapter 12: A Shower of Pintails (Mexico) · 119
Chapter 13: The World's Finest Fowling (Argentina) · · · · · · · · · · · · · · · · · 127
Chapter 14: Wings Over the Pampas (Argentina) · 135
Chapter 15: Alberto's Time (Uruguay) · 143
Chapter 16: Andean Magic (Ecuador) · 149
Chapter 17: The Pisco Shuffle (Peru) · 155

"If I had to choose, I would rather have birds than airplanes."
—Charles A. Lindberg

Spanning the Globe

"Something lost behind the ranges,
Lost and waiting for you. Go!"
—Rudyard Kipling, *The Explorer*, 1903

AUTHOR'S NOTE

"Hello," the voice on the other end answers.

"Is this Curt . . . Curt Gowdy?" I ask.

"Yes, it is," he answers in his inviting broadcaster's tone that instantly triggers reruns in my mind. Reruns of the show. Any hunter or angler born before Lyndon Johnson took office remembers The American Sportsman as if it were the first televised moon landing. For one hour a week, the most valuable object in our home was the television set. Consensus never came easily in our household, but there was no debate over what we could watch when the show was on.

"I'm writing a book about places to hunt birds around the world, Curt," I say, "and, well, I couldn't think of a better person to write the foreword."

"I'm leaving for Chile next Tuesday. Let's talk more before then . . . but I'd be happy to," he volunteers before I have to grovel.

For 20 years, Gowdy hosted ABC's The American Sportsman series, at the time the second-longest-running major network program, behind only Gunsmoke. Gowdy's distinguished sportscasting career included 12 Emmy Awards, six for his work on The American Sportsman. The groundbreaking series spawned an entire genre of outdoor programs—some of value, others regrettable. None has meant as much to a generation of sportsmen, and no others ever could.

When a young television producer by the name of Roone Arledge asked me to host a fly-fishing competition in Argentina for ABC's Wide World of Sports, I had no idea the assignment would lead to a 20-year tour of the globe. What a wonderful journey it was. From the response to that first special, it was clear that American outdoorsmen were eager for a show that celebrated the adventure of the sporting life.

My love of the outdoors came from my father and was nurtured throughout my formative years in Wyoming. In the 1930s and '40s, there were no jet planes, and the highways in the state were gravel. There were only about 200,000 people in all of Wyoming, so the entire state was an outdoor playground—a playground I frequented with shotgun and fly rod in hand.

When I went off to university in Laramie, I remember heading to the duck blind in the autumn before my 8:00 A.M. class. My friends and I would divide our time between sitting in blinds and heading to the creeks, where we'd jump-shoot ducks. Little did I know that the outdoors was perhaps the most valuable classroom I would ever come to occupy.

The world of the outdoors is full of adventure—whether at home or abroad—but viewers loved to dream as our television crew took people along in search of the world's best

hunting and angling. Who could forget stars like Bing Crosby and Phil Harris, two of the finest gentlemen ever to call themselves sportsmen? Many viewers remember the two of them in a sandgrouse blind near Lake Tanganyika. The spectacular hunting became secondary to their entertaining personalities. With such eloquent spokesmen, it was easy for viewers—even if they were nonhunters—to embrace the sport. Many people recall the two of them in Iowa, hunting pheasants on a cold winter day. No one could guess how many birds they got, but those who watched that show can't forget the camaraderie of the two old friends. That's what made the show so special, and that's what makes hunting memorable as well.

If it wasn't guests like Bing and Phil stealing the show, it was the dogs doing the same. I remember telling Bear Bryant, the legendary University of Alabama football coach, that he wasn't going to be the star of the quail hunting show we filmed with him. He was upstaged by a national champion pointer, a dog that moved like wind through cover. In California, it was a Labrador retriever—not home-run king Hank Aaron—that made a duck hunting show so memorable. Skilled dogs make good wingshooting shows—it's that simple. These were dogs for which any bird hunter would trade his last shotgun to own.

People often ask me to name my favorite wingshooting destination. I don't hesitate when I tell them Argentina—anyone who has ever witnessed the endless flights of Magellan geese would agree. It's been more than 30 years since I first made a trip to Argentina, but I keep going back because there's no place on Earth quite like it.

If you take the right frame of mind with you, however, you'll discover that every place is special in one way or another. I loved the goose hunting in Maryland, for instance, because it is a region where waterfowling traditions run deep. I also remember a duck hunt we filmed in Colorado. It was an especially cold day, and one of the few places that wasn't frozen was a natural hot springs that attracted every duck in the vicinity. I'll never forget the way mallards descended on us, their forms materializing through the steam rising from the springs.

No matter where I travel, I always enjoy learning about other lands, for a person who does not explore is missing an important education. The intrigue of an area was part of what we always strived to capture on the show, and that's one of the reasons the series had a lasting impact for so many sportsmen. I remember when I began hosting The American Sportsman, Roone Arledge told me that this

Curt Gowdy and racing legend Jackie Stewart survey the moors during a Scottish grouse hunt. Gowdy taught a generation of American sportsmen to treasure and protect our wild heritage. By hosting ABC's The American Sportsman series, he popularized international sporting travel like never before.

show would bring me more recognition than all the Super Bowls or World Series I would ever cover . . . he was right.

I've seen a lot of changes in hunting and angling over the years. I remember the limit of trout in Wyoming was 20 a day when I was a kid. I also recall wondering why my father would only take a couple of fish home when the law allowed for so many more in our creel. Without pause, he reminded me of the buffalo . . . if they could be wiped out, he said, anything could be overcaught or overhunted.

It's a lesson I've carried with me and shared with my sons. It's a legacy to remember no matter how far we travel and no matter how limitless the game might appear. Indeed, remember the buffalo.

—Curt Gowdy, May 2002

Acknowledgments

I am one of a generation of sportsmen who first set our gaze on distant covers through the images brought to us by Curt Gowdy and *The American Sportsman* television series. No show before or since has captured the essence of adventure any better. Curt, Bing Crosby, Phil Harris, or a cast of other characters transformed the small screen into a window into another realm. It was a world I one day would come to roam.

The essays in this book represent 12 years of traveling the globe with a shotgun and a thirst for wingshooting. Portions of this book have previously appeared in *Ducks Unlimited, Sports Afield, Sporting Classics, Shooting Sportsman, Double Gun Journal,* and *Wing & Shot.* It is the people—as much as the places—who have made the stories. I am especially indebted to Mike and Suzie Fitzgerald, Mike Harrington, Doug Larsen, and the rest of the team at Frontiers for helping introduce me to the vast world of wing-shooting adventure.

A piece of my heart will always rest in Africa, so that is where I begin my thanks. I share many kindred spirits in South Africa. Alistair McLean comes quickly to mind, because his passion for birds, dogs, and fine shotguns gives us ample common turf to carry on conversations that last two bottles of wine and a glass of port past dinner. I will never forget Alistair the day the Springboks defeated the Kiwis for the

World Cup of Rugby. It was the first time the South Africans were allowed to compete internationally after years of isolation caused by sanctions. Never has one game meant so much to one man and to one nation.

I first met Robin Halse on a cold and windy day in the Eastern Cape's Drakensberg Mountains. Robin's affair with greywing francolin is legendary, so my fascination for staunch pointers and sporty birds sparked a lasting friendship. His good humor, engaging personality, and splendid family made my stay at Carnarvon one of the most memorable of my forays to some 16 countries.

The wine region just north of Cape Town is dotted with elegant Cape Dutch manors and some of Africa's most spectacular scenery. That is probably why Basie Maartens wound up there and explains why he and his wife, Sandra, purchased the Mountain Shadows resort. It was the Cape francolin that first took me to their retreat, but it was the delight of their company that lured me back years later.

My fascination for birds really began—and has endured—because of my fondness for gun dogs. The quality of the dog work I've enjoyed while hunting in Africa is extraordinary. None have been better than those trained by Dave Fowler, a South African pro whose canine teaching is exceeded only by his politically incorrect sense of humor. *Warning: His hunts are intended for mature audiences only.*

A morning in a duck blind in Zululand is an experience few wingshooters will forget—that's especially true if you're hunting with Trevor Comins. It's the only place where crocodiles do the retrieving . . . which explains Trevor's dearth of Labradors.

Everyone should experience a francolin drive that yields an elephant or two or maybe a lion or a family of warthogs—it teaches you to keep one eye on the ground and the other in the sky. That was a lesson Mike Gunn taught me in the Eden known as the Okavango Delta. The former Rhodesian is a skilled hunter and naturalist, the kind of person who enriches any African safari.

Gunn's soul mate in Zimbabwe is Steve Seward. He has an infectious enthusiasm for guns, dogs, and the people who share his love for them. Seward is as good with a rifle as he is a shotgun, a welcome talent when flushing pachyderms.

My foray to Russia would not have been complete without my interpreter, Andre Golubev, and hosts, Dr. Sergei Shushunov, Vasily Popov, and Vladimir Selikhov—a quartet who brought spark and optimism to a land lacking both.

A return trip to Hungary brought a chance to renew my friendship with Gabor Laszlo, a gracious host who is one of Europe's most knowledgeable hunters. His unflappable demeanor and good humor serve him well when coping with the rigors of demanding sports. A finer gentleman I haven't met.

What Jan Vebr lacks in size he compensates for in enthusiasm. My hunt with the robust Czech had as much to do with endurance as it did enjoyment, but any man who hunts with a Dachsund better be tough.

For Ruben del Castillo, hospitality comes naturally. When he opens the doors to his Mexican lodge, wingshooters are welcomed with some of the continent's best duck and dove hunting . . . and you can drink the water.

I tip my hat to one and all and toast that we'll one day meet again.

Setting Sail

often wonder whether I travel to hunt or hunt to travel. Somewhere buried in my atavistic memory is a compulsion to explore—both distant game fields and the covers of my imagination. Wingshooters are forever dreaming of places where birds still darken the sky because, in a remote way, we long to return to the halcyon years of shotgunning—as if it is a place rather than a time.

For most of us, this wanderlust begins as does any other addiction, ever so gradually permeating our lives until it becomes an essential part of our existence. It starts the first time we hop a fence to traverse new territory. Soon we're driving cross-country in a search for unequalled gunning. Ultimately, we find ourselves aboard transatlantic flights to places we once knew only through television screens.

Hunters are optimists, eternally working just one more patch of cover, rounding another bend, or speculating on what successes tomorrow will bring. It is the same enthusiasm we pack with us as we embark on distant journeys; the anticipation of such voyages becomes indistinguishable from the adventure itself.

The traveling sportsman is never satiated, as the combination of memorable venues and challenging birds is limited only by time and creativity. For some, it becomes a race to see much of the world before becoming a part of the planet ourselves—a belief rooted in the axiom that experiences are the only possessions worth owning. The value of such travels comes in sharing them with others who have turned a fascinated eye toward distant covers. Here, then, are my stories.

A new world of sporting travel opportunities awaits wingshooters with an appetite for adventure. There's room for you in this South African duck and goose blind . . . interested?

THE WORLD'S GREATEST WINGSHOOTING DESTINATIONS

XIV

Caveat Emptor: Booking Your Safari
(and Other Hazards of Sporting Travel)

efore embarking on foreign wingshooting forays, I sometimes experience a recurring nightmare. It goes something like this:

My plane lands in Istanbul, Kuala Lumpur, or some such place, sans my guns and luggage. Upon arrival, I'm the only pale face in the crowd and the lone person to speak English. No representative from Castaway Safaris is anywhere to be found, and the only hotel in town doesn't accept American Express. Having been told that I didn't need to exchange currency before disembarking, I find that the locals have never seen greenbacks, nor would they ever consider mere paper as legal tender. Two short men with Soviet-supplied AK-47s and no sense of humor are hovering near me as I stare forlornly at the luggage cart that shows no signs of delivering my bags. The next flight out is in four days. The airport is about to close, and phone lines have been down for three days. I was sold a dream but am living a nightmare.

This scenario has entered my psyche subliminally through both the tales of

Enjoy hunting over quality gun dogs? Then make sure the outfitter you'll be using has a kennel of experienced bird dogs—like this South African pointer—before you find yourself globe-trotting after unruly pups.

1

horror that have been shared by other intrepid wingshooters and my own experiences when traveling abroad. I relate it to you so that when it comes to extending *your* hunting universe, you are sure to temper your enthusiasm with a healthy dose of caution. The following advice should help.

BOOKING AGENTS, OUTFITTERS, AND GUIDES

Once you've decided to book a wingshooting foray away from familiar haunts, you'll need to know how to wade through the reams of information about your destination of choice. Every brochure, advertisement, and magazine article promises a trip of a lifetime—but sometimes it is so memorable because of the misery it delivers rather than the pleasure. Although there are plenty of safe and ethical booking agents, outfitters, and guides from which to choose, the secret lies in distinguishing them from the rest of the herd.

The Role of Each

First, you must understand the role of the booking agent, outfitter, and guide. A good booking agent will not only develop a trip itinerary (ideally, one tailored to your desires) but will also handle all of the details of your journey—from booking airline flights to making

sure your birds are properly delivered to your favorite taxidermist. For these services, the agent takes a percentage of the trip cost. To be certain, a booking agent should take the trepidation out of your trip by handling the details for you. Be leery of agents who ask you to acquire gun permits, book internal flights, handle transfers, and so forth. If the agent doesn't intend to manage the trip, he (or she; many excellent agents, outfitters, or guides are female, but for simplicity's sake all will be referred to as he in this book) should explain that to you before you deliver payment. The most misunderstood term in the sporting travel business is "all inclusive." Find out exactly what a booking agent or outfitter means when he says a hunt package is all inclusive and, as with any other contract, get the agreement in writing. If you haven't used this booking agent before, be sure to research his references just as you would those of an outfitter or guide.

As a general rule, an outfitter coordinates all aspects of the hunt itself—independent of the travel to and from the destination. This person's job is to put you in the best possible position to have success in the field by providing the necessary overhead: lodge or camp and pertinent equipment. He should also make certain your accommodations and meals equal or exceed the advertised standard.

The best outfitters employ quality guides.

These are the people who take you to the field and whose responsibility it is to make sure your hunt is as safe and successful as possible. As a general rule, you tip guides, not outfitters—unless your host serves in both capacities.

Sources of Information about Each

There's no question that the best way to find a worthwhile booking agent, outfitter, or guide is by word of mouth—so long as that word is coming from someone you know and whose opinion you trust. More likely, though, you'll have to rely on other means to locate a quality hunt representative. A magazine ad is one place to start, but bear in mind that this is only a start.

When calling a prospective agent, outfitter, or guide, have a prepared list of questions to ask so that you can avoid any confusion later. How long has he been in business? Is he licensed in the state, province, or country in which he's operating? Is he a member of the region's professional hunter's association? If so, this will serve as a good place to begin your background search because any complaints from his hunters will likely have been filed with such an association. Is he insured in case of an accident? What sort of medical emergency care is available at the destination to which you're headed? In many jurisdic-

No one travels halfway around the world to experience a hassle. Unless, of course, that person didn't do his homework and booked with a fly-by-night outfitter. Check out a prospective outfitter the way you might a future business partner.

tions, guides must be insured before they can be licensed. Ask what percentage of hunters are repeat clients. A high percentage of repeat business indicates a favorable satisfaction rate among customers.

You'll also want to ask for several references. If the agent, outfitter, or guide is reputable, he'll have a long list of satisfied clients who are willing to endorse his operation. Do not assume, however, that all the references presented will speak favorably of the operation. An agent or outfitter might be banking on the fact that you'll never actually contact him. I've been surprised many times by what hunters have had to say about an operation that made the mistake of listing them as references. In many cases, the outfitter neglected to contact the reference for his opinion of his operation and whether or not the hunter would even like to serve as a reference in the first place.

When contacting a reference, ask for specific reactions, not general impressions. Did the hunt live up to its billing? Was the guide safe to hunt with? (Though many guides and outfitters require that you sign a liability waiver in the event of an accident, such releases seldom have any bearing on civil suits.) Were birds abundant? Were accommodations and meals what you expected? Did the guide engage in illegal or unethical activities in your presence? Was the outfit's vehicle, boat, motor, camp, and other equipment well maintained and organized? Were there quality dogs to hunt with? Finally, ask the person if he would pay to hunt with the service again. If not, ask him to give specific reasons for his answer.

If you're hunting in the United States or Canada, check with a local conservation warden to make certain a potential guide doesn't have a history of game violations. There's no sense placing yourself in a compromising position by hunting with a guide whose ethics are questionable. Such guides invite scrutiny by wardens, and their clients are too often unwitting bystanders in game violations.

SHOULD YOU BOOK YOUR OWN TRIP?

A growing number of hunters are choosing to book hunts on their own, bypassing the traditional booking agent route. Thanks to expanded Internet access, faxes, and modems, the world of interactive communications has grown exponentially. Keep in mind, however, that this does not mean that extensive background checks are no longer necessary. To the contrary, if you don't have an experienced booking agent to rely upon, it is even more important to investigate any outfitter with whom you think you might book a hunt.

Finally, ask yourself if the level of service justifies the expense. In the world of guided hunts, you very often get what you pay for, and caveat emptor is always the prudent course.

MATCHING THE TRIP WITH YOUR FITNESS LEVEL

Before booking a hunt, make sure you are capable of handling the physical requirements that are part of the activity. There's nothing so sad, in my experience, as watching an elderly or out-of-condition hunter who is unable to cope with the rigors of an expensive, faraway hunt. Too often agents either don't understand the abilities of the hunter or the requirements of the hunt, and the result is frustration on both ends. Conversely, if you're in less than good physical condition, be honest with yourself and your booking agent about your abilities and you'll avoid the pitfall of buying a safari that is too rigorous for you. Moreover, don't use the hunt you booked for Himalayan snow cock as a reason to shed the extra 40 pounds you've been carrying for the past decade. Chances are you won't lose the weight, and ego won't get you up the mountain. Through miscommunication a hunter winds up feeling betrayed and dejected, while the outfitter or guide is frustrated by his inability to deliver gunning success.

KNOW WHAT THE PACKAGE INCLUDES

Make sure the guide informs you—prefer-ably in writing—as to exactly what is included in the cost of the trip. Who pays for shells, hunting license, permits, drinks, meals, and transportation from the nearest airport?

IS THIS A TRIP YOUR SPOUSE WOULD ENJOY?

If you want to bring your spouse along, check to be certain that the facilities will pro-vide a positive experience for both of you. One of the axioms I've learned over years of travel, witnessing marital bliss from continent to continent, is that if the wife isn't happy, she generally makes certain that her husband isn't either.

SHOULD YOU TAKE YOUR DOG?

If you decide you'd like to have your dog with you, ask whether the outfitter or guide has a warm, clean place for it to stay. Is it safe for the dog to hunt a given area? Early-season duck hunts in alligator or crocodile country can be dicey for a dog, and if the guide isn't using a dog, there could be a good reason. Additionally, transporting a dog out of the country can be a far easier proposition than getting it back in. Depending on the nation from which you'll be bringing a dog, quaran-tine periods can last several months.

HEALTH MATTERS

You'll also need to understand health requirements and other travel information before entering a foreign country. Contact the Centers for Disease Control in Atlanta, Georgia, for a listing of necessary vaccinations. Anyone who plans a foreign expedition should also get a copy of *Traveler's Health: How to Stay Healthy All Over the World* by Richard Dawood, M.D. (New York: Random House, 1994), Dr. Dawood is the medical correspondent for *Condé Nast Traveler*, and, to my knowledge, this book is the most thorough compendium of health tips for travelers ever published. By country, this tome lists various diseases, para-sites, snakes, and other hazards a traveler might encounter, as well as precautions to make your stay safe. Your first inclination when reading *Traveler's Health* is to immediate-ly assume that it is risky to venture anywhere. Take necessary steps to make sure you stay healthy abroad but don't fixate on myriad potential hazards awaiting you when traveling, and your trip will be far more enjoyable.

It's a good idea to pack your own first-aid kit anytime you travel—whether domestically or overseas. If you're on medication, you'll need to carry enough to last you for the dura-tion of your trip. I carry an assortment of pre-scription antibiotics ranging from relatively mild to as strong as available—in both cases they're broad-spectrum antibiotics. Explain to your doctor where you'll be heading and whether or not you'll have access to any sort of medical care. Ask if it is possible for him to prescribe a battery of antibiotics, painkillers, and other drugs that might make your tenure abroad healthier and happier—especially if you will not have ready access to medical care while traveling. In addition to antibiotics and painkillers, I carry prescription-strength antidiarrheal medicine as well as drugs to pre-vent vomiting.

In some parts of the wingshooting world, you'll need to take an antimalarial prophylaxis for several weeks before and after your trip. Incidence of chloroquine-resistant malaria has spread in recent years, so many doctors now prescribe new drugs to combat Fansidar-resist-ant falciparum malaria.

Also include a wide assortment of bandag-es, antiseptics (e.g., Betadine, Neosporin), alco-hol wipes, lancets, tweezers, safety pins, scis-sors, hydrocortisone (1 percent), antifungal creams or powders, lip salve (e.g., Carmex, Blistex), aspirin, ibuprofen, antihistamines, motion sickness preventative (e.g., scopolamine patches, Dramamine), sulfacetamide eyedrops, Visine, strong sunscreens, antacids, vitamins, insect repellents, ear plugs, and extra eyeglasses, shooting glasses, or contact lenses.

I also pack a supply of melatonin when I travel. Melatonin is a naturally occurring hormone produced by the pineal gland in the brain. It is responsible for sleep rhythms and has been heralded as something of a miracle cure for jet lag. In my own limited experience, I contend that it has helped me reset my internal clock when traveling across several time zones. The upshot is that it takes me less time to overcome the effects of jet lag. Melatonin is widely available over the counter at pharmacies and most grocery stores.

If you become extremely ill or injured while abroad, you might have to be evacuated for emergency medical care, which can be very expensive. You can buy a separate insurance policy in advance to pay these emergency costs but check first to make sure your individual coverage doesn't already cover you in foreign countries. Trips purchased with certain credit cards automatically provide insurance abroad and will sometimes pay for medical evacuation as well. The key is to know what you already have before you purchase additional coverage. The better booking agents will automatically provide travel insurance as part of their pack-

age. If you're uncomfortable with your level of protection, however, and want to purchase an emergency evacuation policy, contact USAssist (800/225-5911), Access America (800/284-8300), or International SOS Assistance (800/523-8930) for details and pricing.

BRINGING BIRDS BACK

It is legal to import game birds if the birds (1) were taken legally in another country (a license is normally required as proof of such) and (2) do not appear on either Appendix 1 of the Convention on International Trade in Endangered Species (CITES) list or the U.S. Endangered Species list. For more details about both lists, contact the U.S. Fish and Wildlife Service, Division of Law Enforcement, 4401 N. Fairfax Drive, Arlington, VA 22203.

When bringing frozen birds back, you must show U.S. Department of Agriculture (USDA) or U.S. Fish and Wildlife Service officials your customs declaration forms that indicate you're bringing whole birds back for taxidermy purposes. Upon clearing customs, you are then required to ship the birds directly to a federally approved taxidermist. These are taxidermists who have met the necessary USDA requirements of being able to properly dispose of carcasses to prevent the potential spread of disease. For a list of federally approved taxi-

dermists, write the USDA, Veterinary Services, Import/Export Products Staff, 6505 Belcrest Road, Hyattsville, MD 20782.

HAVE GUN, WILL TRAVEL

When traveling to destinations where high volume shooting is a potential, be prepared to cope with excessive recoil. While few American bird hunters ever experience such shooting, that is often not the case abroad—especially on dove fields in such places as Uruguay, Colombia, Argentina, or during driven shoots in such places as England, Scotland, and Hungary. Bringing the appropriate recoil pads and choosing the right gun and loads can make a world of difference in your enjoyment.

Keep in mind, however, that it is often difficult to obtain shotshells other than 12- or 20-gauge. In many cases—such as South Africa, for instance—even 20-gauge ammunition is both tough to find and expensive. Make sure your outfitter understands exactly what kind of shells you'll be needing. It's also a wise idea to bring two guns in case one fails during the shoot. A full set of choke tubes and multiple choke wrenches also should be part of your gunning battery.

Never count on an outfitter having necessary gun-cleaning equipment—pack a modest kit just in case. Gun repair kits also are available for several popular shotgun models, so check at your local gun store for those items. Also ask your gunsmith what parts on the guns you plan to take with you are most likely to break. Pack those spare parts, if possible, and enjoy your trip knowing that you're prepared for almost any contingency.

Last, select a gun case worthy of your safari—in other words, don't trust your guns to flimsy plastic cases. Furthermore, many savvy wingshooting travelers cleverly disguise their guns by packing them in contraptions that don't resemble traditional gun cases. One friend uses an octagonal surveyor's case and has "precision hole drilling equipment" stenciled on the side of it—a little poetic license is acceptable under such circumstances.

Many double gun fanciers favor the gun duffels that several manufacturers are currently making. These bags are handy because they allow you to combine a duffel with a gun case to keep the number of checked bags to a minimum. Don't think for a minute, however, that your gun case is now disguised. In fact, savvy thieves have already caught on to the fact that expensive double guns are often transported in such duffels. You should fully insure your guns with a separate rider policy and take precautions to safeguard against your guns being lost or stolen. Ultimately, however, you must surrender them to the whims of the airlines if you want to use them when traveling.

Part One

Revelry in the Old World

Nowhere is the tapestry of bird shooting more tightly woven and colorful than in the British Isles and on the continent of Europe. While many think of the driven shoots of England and Scotland when conversations turn to bird shooting in Europe, the reality is that *battues* were popular in the former Austro-Hungarian Empire long before the rise of the famed Edwardian shooting parties of the mid-19th century. Rough shooting for pheasants, partridges, hares, ducks, snipe, and even kingfishers and songbirds also existed throughout parts of Europe from Persia to the Mediterranean to France.

It wasn't until two key technological advances came to pass nearly simultaneously, however, that the modern driven shoot began to take shape in England. First was the growth in rail lines criss-crossing the once remote British countryside. The ease with which urban socialites could then travel to scattered estates made it possible to readily accept invitations to lavish shoots in the hinterlands without fear of leaving London-based businesses unattended for long.

Although early trains were primitive affairs that lacked even rudimentary comfort, beginning in the mid-1800s there was a growing demand for luxury cars to accommodate

the English elite. That interest coincided with rapid improvements in both firearms and powder. About 1850, muzzleloading hammerguns gave way to the first breech-loading models. The change in firearms brought about the capability of taking large numbers of birds in a short time—the recipe that would make future driven shoots possible. The chance for such shoots was further improved in 1870, when hammerless guns and smokeless powder were introduced. Smokeless powder was an especially significant advancement because no longer would a cloud of smoke temporarily blind a shooter and prevent the chance of connecting on a quick double in the heat of a productive beat.

Technology facilitated the birth of the modern driven shoot, but it was the social appeal that fueled the growing interest in the sport. By the second half of the 19th century, one's status in the English hierarchy could be clearly determined by reviewing the invitation rosters to the most prestigious shoots. The most lavish shoots were replete with staggering numbers of birds, gourmet field lunches, and live music among the heather. Hosts continually vied for the honor of having produced the shoots with the most and best birds, dining rivaled only by the finest London restaurants, and entertainment more engaging than anything found at other shoots. Dress for such affairs was nearly as formal as for any royal function of the day. Women also partook in the shoots, often attending the gunning galas draped in furs and extravagant jewelry. To be sure, the shoots were a celebration of excess, perhaps the greatest example of hedonism since the great Greek orgies.

Competition continually refined these social affairs, and word of the blasts spread across the continent of Europe, where lords and ladies from far and wide came to sample the British shoots. Royalty from Slovakia, Persia, Russia, Germany, Hungary, Spain, and France found elements of the British shoots that they chose to import to their native lands—whether it applied to pheasants, ducks, partridges, or other game found in their home regions.

Today, wingshooters can enjoy a wide variety of both rough shooting and driven gunning throughout the United Kingdom and the European mainland. A subculture of elite gunners still relishes these shoots, but driven can also be had for comparatively little money today. The British Isles remains the most popular destination for driven birds: red grouse, pheasants, and Hungarian partridges. Spain's red-legged partridge shoots have a reputation of being among the sportiest of any such affairs offered any-

where. I've enjoyed quality driven-pheasant shooting in both Hungary and the Czech Republic, countries to which some driven aficionados cast a disparaging eye for the lack of high-flying birds. Such was not the case during my shoots; the birds I encountered in both countries compared favorably with those found during my shoots in the United Kingdom and Denmark.

A country lacking the legendary driven custom of many of its European counterparts is Denmark. Although the nation's flat plain doesn't feature the topography to drive birds off hills for added challenge, Danish gamekeepers have learned to compensate for the dearth of varied terrain by using tree lines and other obstructions to force birds to fly higher into the air. Flighted mallards also are a popular attraction for visiting gunners to Denmark. The ducks offer a very different kind of shooting and are able to change their flight path far more aerobatically than pheasants, so shooting the two in combination is a sport unrivaled in the driven world.

Both England and Scotland offer elegant driven affairs that can stretch nearly any shooting budget. One of the most exquisite is offered aboard the *Royal Scotsman*, rail travel reminiscent of the heyday of the turn-of-the-century British driven shoots. Although modern-day grouse populations have fluctuated widely, a driven grouse shooter sits highest on the bird-shooting food chain because of the premium placed on this wild game.

The continent, however, offers so much more to the bird hunter. Across Scandinavia, driven capercaillie (the world's largest grouse) gunning is often combined with moose shooting—just be sure to use enough gun. Capercaillie, black cock, woodcock, and ducks can all be hunted in a brief spring season in Russia, providing some of the most intriguing of all shotgun sport.

Whether driven gunning or rough shooting, U.S. wingshooting travelers will encounter a world of opportunity and plenty of kindred spirits across the Atlantic. It's closer than you think.

Black-billed capercaillie (Tetrao urogallus).

Grouse of Another Time

～ RUSSIA ～

A gruff Russian voice rouses me out of my slumber at 2 A.M. like some sort of knuckle dragger sent to interrogate Francis Gary Powers. I am beginning to understand what writer, sportsman, and world traveler Robert Ruark meant when he wrote that it takes time for a soul to catch up to its body after a transatlantic flight, a displaced sensation that he felt upon landing in Africa on safari. When traveling halfway around the planet, time, indeed, becomes a relative term.

Downstairs, in a chorus of laughter, a half-dozen Italian waterfowlers celebrate the success of their hunt by joining in the Russian national pastime of vodka tasting. The hour is either early or late depending on the amount of vodka on the table, your frame of mind, or the time zone you call home. In a haze, I collect my shotgun, hip boots, coat, shells, and thoughts, and amble downstairs. Awaiting me is a cup of coffee and my Russian chauffeur, who will take me to the forest haunts home to capercaillie, an ancient beast that is the Old World's largest grouse.

The capercaillie—a turkey-sized bird with an eaglelike head, slate-gray body,

A male capercaillie displaying in a pinewood habitat. The capercaillie is the world's largest grouse and is among the most coveted of all trophies in Europe. (Photo by Neil McIntyre.)

A German hunter who has come to Russia to stalk the capercaillie. The birds thrived throughout his native country prior to World War II.

and sweeping tail fan—is legendary in the annals of European hunting. It's something of an evolutionary throwback, having remained unchanged for millennia. Its Latin name, *Tetrao urogallus*, loosely translated, means "ancient one." Capercaillie have remarkably outsized curved beaks, seemingly grossly overdeveloped for plucking pine needles, the mainstay of their diets. When capercaillie could still be widely found throughout western Europe prior to World War II, there was a one-in-a-lifetime limit placed on them. Today, the coniferous forests of northern Europe harbor the greatest numbers of the birds.

In terms of territory, Russia is the largest nation on Earth, with a land mass nearly twice that of Canada, and by virtue of its enormity holds much of the planet's supply of capercaillie. For many European sports, a capercaillie is among the world's most coveted trophies. For bird hunters the world over, it simply has no rival.

The uniqueness of the experience is still catching up to me somewhere over the Atlantic as I ride with my strong-jawed, Leninesque driver through the dark northern forests. He speaks no English, and at this hour, neither do I. After 20 minutes of driving over twisting roads, we arrive at the banks of the Burnaja River near its confluence with Lake Ladoga, a 7,000-square-mile

My first capercaillie, a Russian cock taken north of St. Petersburg. It's a momentous occasion in the life of anyone who reveres game birds and game bird hunting.

inland sea that is the largest body of freshwater in Europe.

A series of bonfires lines the bank of the
river like makeshift lighthouses. I watch
through binoculars as the silhouette of a fisherman drinks from a bottle, staggers next to the
bank, and dips a long-handled net into the current. I learn later that he is seining for smelt, a
rite of spring similar to that practiced in my
native state of Wisconsin. The only difference,
as far as I can discern, is that the Russians are
still able to stand at the end of the night.

Greeting me through the darkness is a
jovial thirtysomething fisherman, who I discover later is a former captain in the Russian
navy. He speaks little English and shouts the
few words he does know as if hollering to
one of his comrades over the drone of ship
turbines. The effect is intimidating in the
quiet of the predawn darkness. He directs
me to a small boat that will transport me
across the calm inlet. On the other side
waits Nicolai Kuzmin, a 25-year-old biologist
whose English is considerably better than
my Russian—it took me the better part of a
semester to merely grasp the difficult
Russian alphabet.

We board another Niva four-wheel drive, a
jeeplike vehicle that is remarkably effective at
negotiating foot-deep mud and stumps. The
forest in which we are about to hunt is part of

a 150,000-acre reserve that was retaken from
Finland in a territorial dispute in 1939. In the
headlights the eerie forms of blown-up anti-
tank bunkers loom as if we were on maneuvers behind enemy lines.

Temperatures have climbed in recent
days to the 70s, and the snow is quickly
melting throughout the moss-carpeted forest.
The runoff makes the dirt roads through the
timber appear like woodland streams.
Because of its northern location, the forest is
covered in snow much of the year, or as one
Russian put it: "We have nine months of
winter here, and we spend the other three
months waiting for summer."

We travel for 20 minutes, coming to a
high spot in the forest. Nicolai nods that it's
time to get out. It's 3:15 A.M., and a full moon
sheds what little light there is in the forest. I
grab my turkey gun, inject a pair of magnum
2 x 6 loads into it, and join Nicolai in a slow
walk down a winding path. I remember that
there are brown bears in the area and slip the
gun off my shoulder, trying not to appear
edgy to Nicolai.

The evening before, my interpreter Andre
Golubev—with great animation inspired by
several shots of vodka followed by beer
chasers—acted out the events of a typical
capercaillie stalk. One must listen for the subtle and peculiar call of cock capercaillie, a

sound that is said to possess an almost mysti-
cal quality. From their treetop roosts, capercaillie emit a series of clicking noises that
build to a crescendo before making a sound
that is often described as that of a person rap-
idly sharpening a knife on a steel. When making the final part of the call, an utterance that
lasts perhaps four or five seconds, the bird
becomes momentarily deaf. Glands within the
bird's ears swell at this instant, effectively
becoming earplugs.

It's during this brief period that a hunter
must take two or three quick steps toward the
bird. Following the capercaillie two-step, a
hunter then has to remain perfectly still. Once
the bird finishes its call, it regains its acute
hearing and will spook at the first hint of
movement or a suspicious-sounding twig snap.

Perhaps 400 yards from the Niva, Nicolai
pauses in midstride and reaches his hand out
in front of me. He cocks his head to one side
to listen to a sound I cannot yet discern. In a
few seconds, he points ahead, turns to me, and
affirms the presence of a bird with a nod. We
move in the direction he pointed, pausing
every 40 yards to listen for the bird's call. This
time I hear the bird's eerie notes, looking at
Nicolai just as he pans to me. The bird is still
several hundred yards distant, so we gingerly
slide and tiptoe over the crusty ice patches left
in the thawing woods.

As we step within 300 yards of the bird, Nicolai pauses suddenly like a cat about to pounce. He waits until the bird makes the "sharpening" portion of its call and waves me ahead as he takes two quick leaps toward the sound. The game of hopscotch continues for 20 minutes; we develop an almost rhythmic cadence as the bird seems eager to proclaim its territory to any available hens.

Seemingly very close to the bird—its subtle call makes it difficult to discern its precise location—Nicolai signals me to go on without him. I wait for the bird to call again and continue shuffling toward it. Between the aerobic hops and the drama of the moment, my pulse begins to keep beat on my eardrums. I scan the forest canopy, but shadows swallow the dark form of the bird, keeping it hidden from view.

It calls again, however, and I spy its movement as it tilts its head back and fans its tail. It's sitting on a thick branch perhaps 30 feet up an ancient pine in front of me. I remind myself to shoot when it makes its metallic-sounding call, advice Nicolai shared during our

No trip to Russia would be complete without touring the stunning architecture found in St. Petersburg, the country's most colorful and dramatic city.

drive through the forest. The reason is this: If a hunter shoots and misses while a bird is making the final notes of its call, there's a chance the shot will go unnoticed by the deaf cock, making a second shot possible.

I rise up to aim at exactly the right moment and realize that it's too dark to see the bead of my gun against the dark bird silhouetted by the pine. I remain motionless, pointing my gun to the sky like a Scottish sport waiting in a butt for high incoming grouse. The bird calls again, and I mount the gun to my shoulder and point it toward the faint light of the open sky in an attempt to see if my eye is aligned with the bead of the gun. The mount seems adequate, so I quickly swing back to the semi-visible grouse and fire, sending the bird flushing out of the tree. I shoot again as the bird crosses an opening in the canopy some 40 yards away. It flinches as though it's been hit, but when I dash to the area where I'd last seen the bird, there is nothing but silence. Nicolai sprints toward me as I shoot but is still some 30 yards behind. Within a few seconds, I notice him bolt perhaps 20

May Day celebrations coincide with capercaillie season in Russia. The country lost a staggering 20 million of its sons and daughters in World War II. War survivors make certain the next generation of Russians understand the sacrifices of their forefathers during a somber ceremony in the shadow of a St. Petersburg war memorial.

Spanish have seized the opportunity to explore behind the rusting Iron Curtain.

With time to spare, I venture back to the woods for a sunset woodcock hunt—the European version of the bird I logged countless hours pursuing during my collegiate days in Wisconsin. While the European woodcock closely resembles its North American cousin, it's considerably larger and, because of that, lacks the batlike aerobatics of our woodcock.

Hunting these birds in the spring, I come to find, is more akin to pass-shooting ducks than it is to traditional American rough shooting. We head to a forest opening perhaps 5 acres in size. Through the use of finger pointing and head nods, my guide positions me at the edge of a clearing, where we begin our evening vigil. I glance back at my host, who is checking his watch as though the birds are late for an appointment.

From behind us, I hear a strange coughing sound. Excited, my guide hurriedly taps my shoulder, pointing at the coughing bird as it approaches. It is, indeed, our quarry, but it is too high to try with the light loads I am shooting. No matter, however, as my guide tosses his beret into the air, causing the woodcock to suddenly dive toward the hat for a closer inspection. Containing my laughter and amazement at such peculiar behavior (the bird's, not the guide's), I seize the opportunity

A mixed bag of blackcock and woodcock are part of the spring hunting opportunities found throughout northern Russia.

feet to his left, waving me toward him with a smile. There at his feet rests the capercaillie, killed by two golden pellets to the neck.

I slap Nicolai on the back while hoisting the bird skyward to get a better look at it. Nicolai grew up joining his father on capercaillie hunts in the Ural Mountains, but he has never taken one, so he inspects the specimen as closely as I do. After a moment of repose and reflection, I begin retracing my morning journey all the way back to the lodge near the village of Sosnova.

The two-story brick and stone lodge was built as a sporting retreat for Communist Party officials in 1957. By Western standards, it is a comfortable dwelling but not extravagant. The main entry of the building is lined with mounts of indigenous game—an enormous boar, several wolf and brown bear rugs, and an assortment of ducks and other water birds from nearby marshes. A capercaillie mount greets hunters who step into the dining hall and, in an adjoining room, rests a Russian billiard table.

I sit down to brunch with Andre and the three partners of the Russian Hunting Agency: Vasily Popov, Vladimir Selikhov, and Dr. Sergei Shushunov, a Russian expatriate who immigrated to the United States 15 years ago. Also joining us are a pair of German hunters: Dr. Jurgen Vocke, president of the Bavarian

Hunting Association, and Peter Sieben, a German outdoor magazine editor. While there are still few capercaillie in Germany, there has been no hunting for the birds since World War II. Because of Russia's vast wildlife wealth, the Germans, Italians, French, and

to snuff the bird about 40 yards out. The Russian hat-trick method of woodcock hunting takes advantage of the woodcock's natural curiosity as males fly about in search of receptive females that often advertise their availability by making short leap-flights.

As though the woodcocking hour were upon us, several of the coughing birds began flying transects over the woodlands, waiting for hens to answer their calls. Several more 'cocks find themselves centered in my pattern of eights, completing one of the oddest wing-shooting experiences I've encountered on four continents. Before bidding farewell to Russia and her expansive forests that stretch some 6,000 miles and 11 time zones through much of Europe and Asia, I return to St. Petersburg for a three-day tour.

This city of nearly 5 million inhabitants is second only to Moscow in size and is unquestionably one of Europe's most stunning destinations. The dramatic architecture and beautiful vistas throughout the city are nearly as memorable as the hunting, and combining the two makes Russia perhaps the last great frontier of both sport and culture.

A fully mature capercaillie in its courtship display. Note the white diamond on the top of the cock's wings— this mark is found only on adult cocks.
(Photo by Neil McIntyre)

Ring-necked pheasant (Phasianus colchicus).

CHAPTER 2

A Magyar Revival
～ HUNGARY ～

I t had been nearly 10 years since I'd ambled through the Castle District of Budapest, a vagabond college student taking a respite from a summer of studying the European approach to environmental problem solving. It was amid the city's glorious architecture that I stumbled across the secluded office of a communist-run sporting cooperative, an enterprise that controlled nearly 90 percent of all the hunting in this game-rich nation. Inside the door stood Dr. Gabor Laszlo, a tall, slender man in his early 40s who served as director of international affairs for the cooperative.

Despite my unannounced presence, he pretends to enjoy the barrage of questions I pose to him about the sporting history of Hungary. Three hours and countless anecdotes later, I bid farewell, hoping one day to hunt with him in his native land. That chance was made possible in large part by the fall of communism, the political plague that excelled at little other than crippling the human spirit. The death of Marx's pipe dream was greeted like a cure for smallpox, and new life has brought a surge in private enterprise throughout Hungary and much of the Eastern bloc. It was all the

Thanks to an influx of foreign currency, Hungary has built an impressive infrastructure for visiting shooters. Quality lodges and exquisite cuisine make the country an ideal destination for htis and her parties.

inspiration Laszlo needed to form his own hunting enterprise. Since he was already well connected throughout Hungary and the rest of the European sporting community, his new Vador hunting service was quickly welcomed by foreign sports who were already familiar with Hungary's impressive diversity of excellent hunting.

Germans, Italians, and Austrians make up most of the hunters venturing to Hungary. Few Americans have yet discovered firsthand the bounty of both big game and wingshooting opportunities in this land of diverse habitats ranging from plains to mountains. The country's rich alluvial soils, along with careful management, have helped produce some of the world's best fallow deer and red stags. Driven pheasant shooting is also still a celebrated ritual here, an event with ties

to the days when such endeavors were reserved for the kingdom's royalty. What sportsman who revels in the art of shooting flying hasn't longed at some time for the taste and pageantry of the legendary driven shoot?

After seven hours of flying from New York, I find myself seated across from Gabor once again. Between us is an ornately carved wooden table in one of Budapest's many colorful bistros. Gabor and I renew our acquaintance as he fills my glass with one of Hungary's robust vintages and tells me of the changes since *perestroika*. By the time we finish our traditional Hungarian dinner of goose liver and paprika fish chowder, my thoughts turn to the majesty of the shooting fields that await.

Above: Part of the appeal of worldwide wingshooting is the chance to explore the culinary habitats of some of the planet's finest restaurants. In this case, our driven shooting party begins our foray to Hungary with dinner at Budapest's world-famous Gundel. It's a century-old luxury restaurant that routinely hosts royalty from around the world.

Right: Live entertainment mixes well with cocktails before dinner at a classic Hungarian lodge. The American driven shooting party is hosted by Dr. Gabor Laszlo, an affable man with a lifetime of experience organizing hunting in Hungary.

The next evening, I join Gabor's first group of American sports, seven hunters from the West Coast and their wives. We meet the group for a dinner of native game at the world-famous Gundel, a 100-year-old Budapest restaurant with a guest list that reads like a who's who of European royalty. Indeed, dining at this landmark is more an event than a meal.

From Budapest we board a chartered bus and drive east to the town of Debrecen, near the Romanian border. There, nestled in a poplar forest, is the four-story lodge that will serve as home for three days of shooting. Inside the immaculate chalet, rows of fallow deer and roebuck antlers line the whitewashed walls, a decoration that is the hallmark of every European hunting lodge I've ever entered. The fireplace glows with flickering flames, and the amber light dances off the walls like aurora borealis against an Arctic sky. There is, in a moment of splendor, something universally inviting about a fire, and we are soon mesmerized by its hypnotic powers.

We arrive in November, a bit early for the best driven shooting. In December and January, the weather is colder, and the birds will have had more time to develop both their flight muscles and primary feathers. The pheasants are released in May or June when only six weeks of age and, remarkably, upwards of 80 percent of the birds will survive until the driven shoots. A relentless predator-control campaign accounts for the high rate of survival among these stocked pheasants. In contrast, several studies conducted on pheasants in the United States indicate that between 70 and 90 percent of mature ringnecks released for put-and-take hunting will die within two weeks of release, regardless of whether or not they are shot.

Pheasants liberated at an early age also are more apt to become stronger flying birds because they won't have netting over their heads to hinder the short leap-flights that mark their introduction to flying. The quality of a driven shoot is often judged on the vol-

Pandemonium with shotguns. In the midst of a drive, it pays to get in rhythm with your loader—the birds will be here and gone in a wingbeat.

ume of birds presented and the challenge to a wingshooter of that presentation. Gamekeepers strive to produce strong birds that will provide difficult targets, and that task has reached something of an art form, whether in the British Isles or on the European continent.

In Hungary, the many hunting associations and cooperative farms scattered across the country specialize in hatching pheasant eggs and raising the birds for gunning. Gabor organizes the shoots with the associations, but he must know months in advance how many guns he will have to accommodate so that there will be enough birds at the scheduled time. He, in effect, becomes a poultry speculator. There is no ready supply of pheasants in Hungary that can be purchased just prior to a driven shoot, so Gabor contracts far in advance to ensure that he will, indeed, have fowl for his shoots.

Part of the allure of the driven pheasant shoot is the chance to enjoy a sport once reserved solely for royalty. Nowhere is this more evident than in the United Kingdom, where an entire social class evolved around the rise of the driven shoot. By the mid-19th century, the advent of the breechloading shotgun made it possible to shoot often grotesque numbers of birds with relative expediency. British author Jonathan Ruffer once described the driven shoot as combining "the opportunities of a . . .

High-flying driven pheasants present unusual and challenging targets for American shotgunners used to the going-away and crossing shots most common in rough shooting.

THE WORLD'S GREATEST WINGSHOOTING DESTINATIONS

24

machine-gunner with an infinitely better lunch."

Most modern shoots, however, are quite modest in comparison to some of the turn-of-the-century extravaganzas—sort of a sampling of what was once done on a much grander scale. Today, what the best shoots lack in volume of birds they atone for in the richness of the celebration, for there is a revelry of the spirit that surrounds the driven shooter who immerses himself in the majesty of this sport.

A bearded chap attired in a wax cotton coat and loden pants signals the start of our first day of shooting with a horn serenade that seems to ring back to the 19th century. I scan down the line of American gunners, who recheck their doubles and practice shouldering their guns in anticipation of the melee. Behind each shooter stands a loader, ready to hand the second gun to the shooter with an earnestness that suggests the rapid pace of the reports are more a matter of national defense than sport. The fields of the driven shoot are habitat to the double gun only. Bringing a pump gun or an autoloader to such an event is akin to driving a station wagon to the Academy Awards.

Threatening clouds cover half the sky in front of the line of shooters, but the morning sun casts a glow from behind us and illuminates the shades of blue and purple in the bruised clouds. Earthward, poplar leaves shimmer in the sun like bronze tears as a few birds fly past the other end of our line of guns. Soon, the sky is peppered with cackling roosters and a smattering of hens, negotiating the air currents and line of shooters in a scene that has changed little over the last century.

The loaders—a group comprising mostly farmers—will not only inject shells quickly into a shooter's second gun, but will synchronize their pace with a gunner so the shoot isn't interrupted. There is a degree of hastiness that overcomes many gunners in a driven shoot as they face the prospect of taking more birds in a day than can be had in an entire season back in the States. The veteran of the driven shoot, however, avoids the temptation of marginal shots, focusing instead on the abundance of higher percentage opportunities. The hallmark of classic driven shooting is the high incoming bird, a litmus test for any gunner who fancies himself a driven shooter.

Dr. William Murray, an orthopedic surgeon from California, and John Lonergan, whose In Transit Travel company arranged the shooting foray for the party, are in the midst of the heaviest flight. The efficiency with which birds fall to their reports is ample indication of their driven shooting experience. Though the loaders speak little English, cheers of "Bravo! Bravo!" follow the shots in a chorus as the loaders can't help but notice the proficiency of the two Americans. It wasn't until later, as I scan down the line to the other shooters in the group, that I notice they also are highly skilled with their shotguns.

One's position on a shoot can mean the difference between spectating and participating, though the best drives provide at least some gunning for everyone on the line. Even at my slowest stand, I find plenty of birds to keep my interest. Numbered posts are set some 40 yards apart at the end of several fields and shooters rotate two positions before each new drive, which is designed to distribute the gunning opportunities.

A typical day of shooting means five or six drives with a civil break at noon for a tempting lunch featuring such entrees as roast venison in a red wine sauce, a dish that alters one's perception of hunting lodge cuisine. Indeed, a classic driven shoot is the dessert of a fortunate wingshooter's life: a hedonistic event that is best savored, like anything of unabashed pleasure.

Before embarking on the afternoon shoot, we sit in a semicircle around the fireplace in the lodge, ruminating over the morning's encounters and pondering the afternoon forays that will again be graced with the mesmerizing cackles of countless roosters. The afternoon pace slows with the thirst for activity largely quenched by the morning flurry. Laszlo dispenses Nike cartridges to us as my loader, Tibor Fejes, fills a leather pouch with

Collecting the spoils of the day. The birds will be taken to nearby markets and sold to a population that's not squeamish about consuming game. In fact, the birds are most often sold feathers on.

the shells. The thirtysomething Hungarian, like his fellow loaders, is a sturdy sort with a ruddy complexion that hints of a life spent on the land. The Hungarian-made shells are of

high quality. Nike is a Hungarian abbreviation for Nitro-Kemia (or Nitro-Chemical), the only company to manufacture shotgun shells in the country. Nike purchased its reloading

Walking between drives in the pastoral Hungarian countryside. Each gunner randomly draws for position in the line of guns. Despite such democratic efforts, occasionally a gunner will enjoy the hottest stands throughout the day.

equipment from Fiocchi, the well-known Italian shotshell manufacturer.

Once again the 25 beaters begin their procession, their whoops and whistles sounding like the gallery at a bullfight. Despite the shooting mayhem that is a normal part of a drive, gunners are always cautioned not to shoot too low, sparing the beaters a shower of falling pellets . . . or worse. Protocol varies from shoot to shoot, but it's perfectly acceptable during most such events to take birds behind you by simply turning your back to the beaters and firing as the birds are going away. As the beaters near the line of guns—in most shoots—the horn man will often signal that it is time for the gunners to turn away from the beaters, facing the opposite direction. Here again, shooters take only birds that are going away. This is a precaution to make certain that the beaters live to flush another day.

Beaters begin their work the day before our event, conducting preliminary drives over a vast area to concentrate the birds in numbers sufficient to sustain a driven shoot. The intensive labor requirements and expenses involved in providing a quality driven shoot have become prohibitive in many areas in recent years, making such functions even more cherished than they already were. Like treasured art, the Hungarian driven-shooting experience should be savored for its uniqueness in a world where links to sporting history are forever disappearing.

Ring-necked pheasant (Phasianus colchicus).

Czeching Out the New Republic

CZECH REPUBLIC

hen I first set eyes on Eastern Europe nearly two decades ago, Berlin remained a city divided, Russia still carried a stick large enough to keep its tenuous union in tact, and the police in the streets were there to protect the government instead of the people. Indeed, much has changed since then, and I am eager to see the metamorphosis firsthand.

This time I have the added incentive of visiting my brother Joe, who is on diplomatic assignment to the American Embassy in Prague, the capital of the Czech Republic. After having spent 15 years living and working in places where dogs are more often found on menus than in bird fields, he is eager to step back into the world of bird dogs and wing-shooting—a pastime that was once a way of life for him.

Despite being a lifelong setter devotee, I quickly warm to my brother's newly acquired Munsterlander, a precocious 8-month-old female named Gora, a moniker bestowed by its German breeder. The small Munsterlander originated in northern Germany, where it was known as the *Heidewachtel*, or heathland quail dog. Facially, it resembles a spaniel while its conformation is almost setter-like. Members of this breed are skilled

Czechs, like
Germans,
admire all
manner of
roe deer
antlers. This
collection
represents the
lifetime
achievement
of a Czech
forester.

A midday break to roast sausages and bread that can only be washed down with the Czechs' world-famous Pilsner beer. Hundreds of these community hunt clubs exist across the Czech Republic and create opportunities for hunters to celebrate the social aspects of a hunt.

pointers and robust retrievers, a potent one-two combination. Gora strikes me as remarkably swift and agile in the field, yet is as responsive to commands as any fine German sportster.

We course the patchwork of small farm fields near Prague, a landscape reminiscent of the American Midwest of the 1950s. The parcels are rimmed with wide fence lines that create—by American standards—an abundance of edge cover. It is this habitat, coupled with the fact that hunt clubs regularly release birds throughout the countryside, that largely accounts for the generous pheasant populations found throughout the Czech Republic. The fate of those pheasant populations, however, is uncertain as state-run cooperatives give way to private farms. It seems inevitable that agriculture across the Eastern bloc will likely follow the path of efficient agribusiness taken by the West, but changes on the land occur far more slowly than do even political reforms, so the birds' fate seems secure for the foreseeable future.

Now, however, the overcast skies can't dampen my intrigue at sampling this country's ringneck hunting. I join my brother and nephew, Kevin, as we work the hay and wheat fields outside of Prague, the crown jewel of Eastern Europe's many fabled cities.

A railroad track traverses the middle of the section, and an old engine pulls 20 cars along

Pheasants come in a variety of color schemes across Europe.
The dog in the background is a small Munsterlander, a delightful pointing breed
that appears something of a mix between a spaniel and a setter.

at a lazy pace, their undulating motion created by the gentle waves of the well-traveled bed. The industry of the Czech Republic is in sharp contrast with the agrarian base of the Slovak Republic, the two jurisdictions that once made up Czechoslovakia. Because of the peaceful division of the country (or the "Velvet Revolution" as it's often referred to), there remain close economic ties between the republics, and the rail lines are the threads that make that commerce possible.

Soon after the train leaves the area, we are following Gora as she makes fluid sweeps through the small, grassy patches that punctuate each fence line. A mere 8 months old, the dog is pointing wild pheasants with a mastery well beyond her youth. My fascination with the pheasants is overpowered by my amazement at the prowess of the dog. With each point, I grow increasingly curious as to why this breed is relatively unknown in the States. There are estimated to be fewer than 500 on the entire North American continent, a fact that is particularly astounding when weighed against the natural ability of this breed.

That bird sense is particularly evident when the dog is confronted by a cock pheasant that scampers nearly 400 yards from where the dog first detected the rooster's scent. While many pointers, particularly inexperienced ones, are often wont to simply sprint toward the bird

Each member of the shooting party receives his portion of the day's take—be it fowl or fur.

until flushing it far ahead of the gun, Gora keeps an even tempo. She first locates the bird in a mixed thicket of dense grass and briars—much like the cover you'd find anywhere in the American Midwest—and relocates on point five more times before finally trapping the bird along the edge of a plowed wheat field. Dazzled by the brilliance of the performance, I swing my over-and-under past the flushing bird and pro-ceed to cleanly miss twice. Thanks to Joe's backup, however, there are birds for the table at the end of the day, and I become a full-fledged member of the Munsterlander Society, a fan club to which Europeans have long had the good sense to belong.

ROUGHING IT

We plan a second day of rough shooting for the pheasants and hares, a tandem as tradi-tionally intertwined in the region as are grouse and woodcock in New England or the Great Lakes. The hunt is the first of the season for a club comprising mostly Czech hunters and a few foreign nationals who are allowed to join their ranks with a small infusion of green-backs, francs, and deutsche marks. We meet one of Joe's hunting compatriots, Frenchman Andre Roussel, and make the one-hour drive to the small town of Mirovice, where we greet the other 25 members of the association.

By the time we arrive from Prague the group, dressed in loden coats, hats, and knick-ers, has already assembled along the side of the main street, where they are discussing the impending festivities. As with all forms of hunt-ing in Europe, there is a healthy dose of tradi-tional protocol to follow before the stalk com-mences, and an abridgment of that ceremony is strictly *verboten*. After greeting each shooter with a handshake and a customary tip of the hat, hunt master Jan Vebr informs the row of gunners about the plans for the day's shoot. In a group of this size, safety is an especially important consideration and Vebr's words of caution translate clearly in the tone of his voice alone—even though his language might just as well have been Yiddish for all I could discern.

With Czech-built Brno doubles, Russian-made Baikals, and a smattering of Italian Zolis slung over their shoulders, the detachment marches down the main road leading from the town, looking as though the next stop is the Eastern Front. Soon, however, we are at the edge of the village, and the procession of hunters forms a line across a large field of beets, a habitat I'm told that hares cannot resist. With about 30 yards between shooters, we course the countryside surrounding the quaint villa. Gun reports are heard periodically up and down the line as hares spook from the scant cover. The European hare is a formidable beast, about the size of a stout beagle, and requires a peppy load of well-placed number 2 or 4 shot to subdue it.

Joe soon encounters one at the fringe of the range of his 20 gauge and tickles the hare with two shots. Instead of scampering away perpendicularly from the line of shooters, the hare chooses to run parallel to the row of guns, tempting the fire of several shooters down the line. Unscathed, the hare clears our Maginot Line of sorts and returns to the cover of the beets behind us.

Ahead, in a small plot of woods, several diminutive roe deer scurry across the expanse of the surrounding field that has already been plowed in preparation for the spring planting season. The spaniel-sized deer are much like a European version of whitetails in that they're found almost anywhere that trees and crop fields intersect. Tall high seats tower over the countryside along the edge of forests like tree houses built on a Pentagon budget, stands from which hunters take the abundant roe deer throughout the lengthy hunting season.

We pause shortly before noon at a clearing atop a nearby hill, and the club members build a bonfire from branches gathered from earlier pruning operations. Such a rest is customary on club hunts, and we skewer bulging sausages on sharpened sticks and toast them over the flames as though they are so many marshmallows from our youth. We mix the flavor of the meat with bites of hearty dark bread and wash it down with swallows of Pilsner and Budvar beers. Much is made of the many fine German brews, but beer connoisseurs know that Czech brewmasters concede nothing when it comes to the question of who produces the finest beer in the world.

The animated faces and jubilant tones of the conversations are ample indication of the reverence the hunters have for the chase, much like their brethren a world away. The older members of the club have seen many changes in their lifetimes, and I ponder what they are thinking as they stare into the warming flames, the fear of swastikas and the hammer and sickle dissipating like faded nightmares.

We end the daylong foray with a traditional pheasant shoot, released birds that dot the cover of a grassy valley. Club members share in the responsibility of raising the birds, and they eagerly await the day on which the chores end and the birds become game. Some 150 birds are raised for this season's shooting, and there are a handful of modest shoots planned throughout the autumn. Late in the season, members are allowed to bring their shorthairs, Labs, and a hodgepodge of other breeds to the lands leased by the club and rough-shoot any pheasants that escape the onslaught of hunters craving pheasant goulash.

The conclusion of the hunt is marked by a ceremonial display of game, a rather somber reflection and moment of thankfulness for the success of the hunt. It is a hint of the respect European hunters hold not only for the game they stalk, but also for themselves as sportsmen. Then, as is customary, the hunt master fastidiously places the pheasants and hares in rows and proclaims the tally of the day, distributing the game to the hunters. A dinner with six or seven courses of toasts at a nearby inn completes the experience.

When finished, the sports walk (or stagger) back to their homes in the village, carrying a mixed bag of pheasants and hares . . . and memories. They are, ultimately, like the rest of us who cherish hunting as much for the people it brings us close to as for the game it provides us.

Following the club shoot, the members march to a nearby restaurant for a hot meal and plenty of drink before returning home. The only difference between this and a North American deer camp is the language in which the lies are told.

A GUIDED TOUR
OF KONOPISTE CASTLE

About an hour's drive from Prague sits one of the hunting world's most spectacular attractions. The Konopiste Castle was the home of the late Archduke Franz Ferdinand, heir to the throne of Austria. Ferdinand is most remembered because his assassination was one of the events eventually leading to the outbreak of World War I.

Prior to his death, however, Ferdinand was perhaps the most prolific hunter the world has ever known. During his lifetime, he is purported to have taken an astounding 300,000 animals, about 1 percent of which are now displayed in the Konopiste Castle. The castle was completed in 1319, nearly 30 years after its construction began. Today, the castle houses thousands of priceless artifacts, including hundreds of firearms from the 16th and 17th centuries. Visitors can see guns featuring three different detonation systems: matchlock, wheellock, and flintlock. Some firearms combine different lock systems. One such exquisite piece, made by Nuremberg master Wolf Danner in the 16th century, uses both matchlock and wheellock ignition systems.

In addition to the Danner piece, from the "master of animal head ornaments" (*Meister der Tierkopfranke*) is an ornately carved rifle given to Ferdinand III as a gift upon his marriage to

A short drive outside Prague sits Konopiste Castle, the home of the late Archduke Franz Ferdinand. Purported to be the most prolific "hunter" in the history of the world, Ferdinand took an estimated 300,000 animals in his lifetime. The castle is home to spectacular game mounts and an astonishing collection of historic firearms. (Photo by Dusan Smetana.)

Anna Maria of Spain in 1631. French, Catalonian, and English long guns and pistols with flintlocks are also found in the remarkable collection, including a pair of English pistols from 1593. Other noteworthy guns include a set of rifles, the so-called "tesins." They feature wheellocks and specifically modeled butts decorated by fine ornaments inlaid with carved bone, nacre, or brass plate. They

were made in Silesia from the end of the 16th to the 18th centuries. One piece bears the mark PK—of master Pavel Kalvoda from the mid-17th century.

For anyone with an interest in fine European firearms and hunting, Konopiste Castle is unrivaled. Though the castle is closed during winter months for maintenance, special tours can sometimes be arranged upon request.

CHAPTER 4

Heather or Not
SCOTLAND

he country known for single malts, tartan kilts, and wailing bag-pipes is, at least in the shotgunning world, most celebrated as a premier driven-shooting destination. The undulating moors echo with the sound of double guns intercepting grouse each autumn as they have for more than a century. It is a season marked by gunners slipping into stone butts to await a line of beaters as they push across a lavender sea of heather waving in the island's eternal breeze.

Grouse, however, are fickle. There's no domesticat-ing these birds, so the viability of shoots varies widely from year to year. A string of tough breeding seasons for the grouse in the 1990s made the pheasant shoots all the more inviting to many foreign sports partaking in the pageantry of Scottish driven gunning. Good pheasant beats begin with sound poultry science; the birds are hatched in incubators and raised in pens for several weeks until such time as they're ready to mature in the wild. It is the only way to consistently provide birds for the gun . . . in numbers that stagger the imagination.

Driven shooting, however, is not to be confused with hunting—at least not in

A spaniel waits his turn to mop up the field after a Scottish driven shoot.

the American sense. It will never replace an autumn day spent walking solo with a favorite dog through cover, the feeling of accomplishment at taking a cagey late-season ringneck or grounding a skittish partridge before it's swallowed by a jungle of foliage. It won't be a substitute for a memorable morning in which you had to break ice to reach your duck blind—the same dawn in which flock upon flock of decoying mallards found your decoys. It won't make you forget your early days as a shotgunner either—the electric combination of a Model 12, Winchester AAs, and pigeons flying out of a barn at treetop height.

The wind is blowing about 30 miles an hour and raining horizontally as I join a group of fellow American sports for my first day of driven shooting in Scotland. We're positioned in a shallow valley—just below a steep bank that looks like the result of a generation of erosion from too much rain. The notion is to give the birds added elevation before they take flight over the guns by driving them off such terrain. Despite the deluge that would

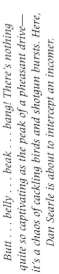

Butt . . . belly . . . beak . . . bang! There's nothing quite so captivating as the peak of a pheasant drive—it's a chaos of cackling birds and shotgun bursts. Here, Dan Searle is about to intercept an incomer.

normally hamper a pheasant's flight, the birds tower above us—first in singles and then in pairs in a steady stream of targets. Steam rises from my gun barrels as the precipitation hits it, making it appear as if it's smoldering. I try to distinguish passing birds from the raindrops that accumulate on my glasses each time I tilt back to fire the second barrel of my Parker. My loader meanwhile, a thirtysomething farmer from the area, snaps two more cartridges into my second gun as a mixture of Hungarian partridge and pheasants suddenly appears from behind the curtain of the hill.

The partridge are deceivers—like minis in a sporting clays course—seemingly flying much faster than their ringneck counterparts. In actuality, however, it is the pheasants that move with greater speed. The small size of the Hun is all that is usually needed to fool most shots. There aren't enough partridge in the drive to comfortably sort out the shots they present—all part of the subterfuge orchestrated by any hunt master worth his kidney pie. Nevertheless, I manage to intercept several birds—mostly by virtue of unleashing enough lead into the air. To my left, Floridian Griff Jenkens shows no signs of suffering from the same inconsistent shooting that I'm demonstrating before my Scottish host, Wilson Young.

The downburst clears in time for our second drive. On the surface, witnessing the first

sunlight of our trip to the island nation might seem a welcome development. That is the case until I draw the stand facing into the 10 A.M. sun—the same direction from which the wind-blown pheasants will appear. I change to darker shooting glasses and raise my hand in a half-hearted salute to the sun to shield its rays from my eyes. The birds begin taking flight, passing through the sun, at which point I lose them until they are just above me and nearly impossible to intercept. I try to finesse my angle away from direct sunlight, but the birds remain little more than sunspots lasered into my pupils.

The beaters work a hillside covered with a copse of trees reminiscent of the windbreaks once so commonly planted by the Civilian Conservation Corps across the American plains following the Dust Bowl years of the 1930s. The birds congregate in this island of cover surrounded by open sheep pasture. As the 15 beaters surround the cover, the birds begin flying toward the guns—sensing no other option of escape. The first bird out is a ridiculously high rooster that appears too far to even attempt a shot. Dan Searle didn't share my view—an unfortunate development for the pheasant. With his first barrel, Searle sends the

The loaders break for kidney pie and hot tea. Inside the Black Bull, the shooters convene for lunch and a round of gentle ribbing about their morning shooting.

bird to earth like a Reggie Robie punt plunging inside the 20-yard line. With no other birds in the air, Searle enjoyed an audience who knew to appreciate such a shot. At his report, a flock of birds lifts from the trees and prompts a mayhem of shooting that lasts for several minutes until hundreds of birds have passed over us. After fighting the sun, my eyes feel as though I've been forced to watch an hour of arc welding.

At the completion of the drive, the clouds and rain return. We retreat to a nearby barn, where Young pours cups of hot consommé as his son, Wilson Jr., tops off the mugs with sherry—Tabasco is optional for anyone having difficulty ridding himself of a chill. It's a perfect chance to informally acquaint ourselves with the rest of the party—a group of friends who have been shooting together for years. Claudia Ball, a widower from Texas and frequent world wingshooting traveler; Griff and Patty Jenkins; Idahoans Mike and Barb Justice; Harry and Taffy Sands from the Bahamas; and Steve Phillips from New York complete this mixed bag of gunners.

A third drive pits me in the midst of a stand of trees, where I have only a very narrow corridor in which to shoot. I begin won-

A star of the event. Soon this handsome bird will be winging his way over a line of shooters waiting with side-by-sides.

dering how I might have irritated Young to be sentenced to such a hidden position.

Nevertheless, I wait to see what might transpire. In a few moments, gun reports begin popping all around me like opening day of duck season on a public hunting area, the birds remaining as yet invisible from my foliage tunnel. I hold my gun at port arms as pheasants begin darting across my field of view in the time it takes to push a safety to the fire position. If there is going to be shooting to be had, I resign myself, I'm going to have to simply react to the birds as if I'm attempting to hit

Above: Dining during a driven shoot is just as formal as the gunning. Driven shooting is about enjoying the very best life can dish out.

Right: Where else can a man wear a dress and not be laughed at? It's often said that a true Scotsman doesn't wear anything under his kilt . . . but no one has ever been brave enough to look.

Above: A skilled loader will continuously keep his gunner supplied with live rounds so that the all-important rhythm of the shoot isn't interrupted during the peak of the flight.

Left: Driven shooting will occasionally test your long-range shooting abilities as well as your sense of humor.

the ruffed grouse of my youth. It works. Call it what you will—snap shooting, instinctive gunning, the Churchill method, a wing and a prayer—the reflexive shots connect, raining poultry all around me as I quench a lustful desire to shoot true. The wingshooter's mantra of butt-belly-beak-bang pays dividends.

We load up the Rover and head back to Burncastle Lodge, a new country home owned by the Duke and Duchess of Northumberland, whose taste in art is evident throughout the manor. Original oils cover the walls of the estate, tucked at the foot of one of the region's finest grouse moors. Inside, the Duke and Duchess' chef prepares a dinner featuring broiled salmon over a watercress and leek sauce followed by crème brûlée. Suddenly, the thought of missed shots escapes me—numbed by the combination of vintage wine and sumptuous food.

Dinners are as formal as the shoots: tweed coats, ties, and "breeks" are as much a part of the culture of the driven shoot as are Wellingtons and double guns—side-by-sides if you care to honor the most traditional protocol. A glass of port around the fireplace following dinner provides the conclusion to a page in a wingshooter's diary that will be dog-eared from being reread time and again.

CHAPTER 5

An Attack of Pheasants
~ DENMARK ~

riven shooting is overindulgence with a shotgun—especially if done right. To be on the moors on the Glorious Twelfth or beneath a cloud of red-legs outside of Madrid or ahead of a line of beaters in Denmark as the pheasants spill out of cover or on stand when a covey of 200 guineas flushes toward you is to have positioned yourself well atop the wingshooting food chain. The driven shoot is about high incomers, the frenzy of so many birds and so little time, the rhythm between loader and gun, staying in the lane, keeping sky below the birds you shoot, game parades, eating better and laughing harder than you ever have in your life. And it's about toasts at the end of the day . . . and more toasts. It's about tradition and civility in a world too often lacking both. Do it enough and it will overcome you like any other addiction.

Most forms of wingshooting share similarities. The dove and duck hunter will know many of the same angles from crossing shots to going-away chances. To the gun, a straight-away pheasant is a departing quail is a disappearing grouse—cover the bird and tap the primer and you stand a good chance of being a bird richer. Conversely, there's nothing quite like a pheasant that towers as it approaches a line of guns in

A preshoot safety lesson keeps gunners under control during some of the most frenetic shooting one will ever experience.

a driven shoot. It is a shot that, in theory, shouldn't confound me. Few sporting clays courses have anything that approximates such a target, for driven pheasants are frequently climbing and gaining speed as they approach—often lulling gunners into overconfidence. That's my story, as they say, and I'm sticking to it.

For Lars and Vinnie Torp, autumn is a chance to share the field with old friends from abroad—some of whom have been coming to Denmark since the Torps first began hosting driven shoots some 20 years ago. In the early days, Denmark was the driven-shooting world's bastard child, since the history and pageantry of the sport lay primarily on the British Isles. Over the course of time, however, the driven-shooting fraternity has not only discovered Denmark as a premier destination, it has embraced it as a place where the birds are strong and more affordable than in the United Kingdom.

Two people largely responsible for Denmark's notoriety in the wingshooting world are Mike and Susie Fitzgerald, who, during the same period of time, have built perhaps the finest reputation in the sporting booking world. Their Frontiers travel company has become synonymous with the best of worldwide wingshooting. My wife, Amy, and I join them for our introduction to Danish shooting . . . and what an introduction it is.

The city of Copenhagen, though a chilly 47 degrees and overcast as we arrive in early November, provides a dramatic passageway to the continent. Like so much of Europe, Copenhagen is rife with history, evident in the rich architecture that adorns this city by the sea. The Hotel D'Angleterre, a dramatic structure in the heart of the city, is our nest for the stay. A private dining veranda encased in glass affords a spectacular view of the bustling city. Danes wrapped in all manner of sweaters and scarves walk past at a brisk pace brought about by the chill in the air. Dinner's featured entrée consists of succulent veal in a reduced red wine sauce.

As is so often the case when I travel, however, I'm anxious to depart civilization and roam the country roads, woodlands, and fields in search of wildlife and other kindred souls with whom I might not share a common language but with whom I share the spirit of the hunter.

Lars is just such a man—though he speaks perfect English, as do most Danes. We board a motorcoach for an-hour-and-a-half drive to a palatial estate adorned with a stone castle-like manor that provides a distinguished backdrop for our day of driven pheasant shooting. What else would you expect in Europe? We board a covered wagon being towed by a tractor that follows trucks carrying beaters and dog handlers—perhaps 20 men and women in all. Given the inordinate amount of rain that has besieged the whole of Europe in recent weeks, the tractor will prove invaluable should extracting a vehicle buried up to its axles become a necessity.

As a seaside country, Denmark is Nebraska-flat with a mixture of hardwood forests and fields that is reminiscent of parts of my native central Wisconsin. The challenge to hunt masters, then, is getting birds to present sporting shots without having the luxury of driving them off hillsides, where they will automatically reach high altitudes as they pass over the shooting line. One solution is to make certain the birds are mature as soon as the season opens, ensuring that they'll have the physical ability to stretch even the best gunner's wingshooting prowess.

Our first drive provides proof that Danish birds hold up favorably when compared to pheasants on the islands. Such a topic is at the center of considerable debate among tested driven shooters, for each has a favorite destination in which to enjoy this legendary pastime—largely based on the quality of the birds that they have encountered. When comparing

By pushing the birds over a row of tall trees, the hunt master is able to force the pheasants to gain altitude before passing over the guns, thus providing highly challenging targets.

(Photo by R. Valentine Atkinson.)

AN ATTACK OF PHEASANTS (DENMARK)

45

driven-shooting opportunities, Denmark provides more birds for less money than one would pay in England, Scotland, or Ireland. Another plus for Denmark is the chance to enjoy voluminous duck shooting—flighted mallards that present a much different target than their gallinacious counterparts. A ringneck will take a direct course over a gunner, whereas a duck, upon being shot at and missed, has the ability to change directions in an instant, flaring out of range before a second barrel can be trained on it. The contrasts in the shots each species provides make a combination shoot one of the most intriguing in all of shotgunning.

When it comes to enjoying hunt cuisine, Denmark surrenders nothing to the British Isles. In fact, one would be hard-pressed to find any dining experiences that surpass what is offered in Denmark—I have two new holes in my belt as proof (and it's not because I've *lost* weight). Game dishes in sauces inspired from local ingredients are perennial favorites. For *foie gras* lovers, too, a visit to Denmark will confirm that the liver is, indeed, the best part of a goose.

With our line of 10 shooters stretching some 200 yards along a woodland composed of a mixed stand of poplar and larch, the beaters descend on an oval of trees and shrubs standing in the midst of a field of sugar beets.

The cover was undoubtedly planted for just such an occasion. A spaniel dislodges a hare that hopscotches past me as the invasion of pheasants begins. A quartet of birds drop with my first four shots as I struggle to contain my confidence—it now seems doubtful that another bird will escape my wrath. My momentary delusion ends as quickly as it arrived, however. I miss the next five shots in succession. An easy hen—a bird that I would have otherwise passed had I not been desperate to rescue my ego—became fodder for my load of steel shot. Only nontoxic shot can be used throughout the nation: Denmark was the first country in the world to ban the use of lead shot entirely.

Several drives yield numbers of birds that can best be described as Hitchcockian—sometimes as many as 200 birds cloud the air above the guns at any one time. The scene is pandemonium as gunners rush their shots—occasionally firing before the guns have even reached their shoulders. They fumble cartridges to the ground as they attempt to load too quickly, as if a wounded buffalo is charging them. Hats often fall off during the best drives because a person is never more agile than when trying to arc back to intercept a bird with the second barrel after it has escaped the first shot. At least I'm assuming others did the same as I did during the peak of the drives—

only a Philistine would divert his eyes from incoming birds at the climax of a beat.

Behind me, a dog handler and a spastic spaniel tend to recovering the birds. All manner of strangely marked breeds are worked throughout the game fields of the Old World. The European approach to game management is more akin to agriculture than wildlife restoration. These pheasants began their lives in an incubator and are raised for the gun and, subsequently, for market. Gunners pay to shoot the birds, not eat them. Pheasants taken during the drives are then sold at market, and it's not uncommon to find a wide variety of game in shops throughout downtown Copenhagen. Unlike Americans, most Europeans don't find poultry with pellet holes in their carcasses offensive, which is to say that they haven't been so domesticated as to lose their sense of place in the web of life.

The last beat of the day finds me at the end of a long row of corn bordering an equally lengthy and narrow woods. Behind me is more forest that will provide flushing birds the perfect place in which to escape. But they must pass over me to get to safety. It is a dream stand, and I am as grateful as a panhandler might be for an unexpected C-note. I move the shell bag ever closer and place extra cartridges in my pockets to be certain that I can make the most of my good fortune. I don't

Pheasants are considered a delicacy throughout the country, so the gamekeeper will have no trouble finding a market for the day's take. (Photo by R. Valentine Atkinson.)

want to disappoint the rest of the shooters, who would undoubtedly be irritated that such a fine position was wasted on a bungling shot.

A trio of diminutive roe deer are the first to bolt past, causing me to flash back five years to the Okavango Delta when a francolin drive flushed six impala, a family of warthogs, and a cow and calf elephant. My daydream doesn't last—something of a covey of pheasants lifts from the edge of the woods, prompted by the yelps and hollers of the beaters. Most of the birds are heading toward me. I focus on the first to enter my airspace, intercepting it at about 40 yards. The second barrel has the chance to complete a double but betrays me instead. I inject two more cartridges, whiffing with both barrels as I train my eyes on a long-tailed rooster, but my gun is too slow to catch up. Redemption comes with the next four shots, connecting on a pair of doubles. My peripheral vision catches the rest of the line in various stages of chaos, birds dropping from the sky like so many plumed coconuts shaken loose in a gale.

While two guns and a loader are common-ly employed during British shoots, Danish driven consists of one gun sans a loader, unless specially requested. With such a volume of opportunity, it's hard to feel cheated by the lack of a loader and an additional gun. Given the numbers of birds harvested during these shoots, an estate seldom hosts more than two or three such events per season.

Alas, the horn sounds, signaling the end of the drive. I peer earthward and see the litter of spent cartridges and wonder who was shooting next to me when I wasn't looking. Soon the dogs are snuffing and prodding the cover behind me, collecting the fallen birds. As is the custom on the continent—not on the British Isles—the pheasants are neatly positioned in rows of hens and cocks adjacent to the manor, where a brief salute to the hunt concludes a day of driven in Denmark.

And what a day it was.

Part Two

Safari Wings

When Sir William Cornwallis set sail to Africa's Cape Colony to convalesce after being stricken with fever in 1836, he set into motion a chain of events that began the grandest age of hunting the world has ever known. His interest in hunting—off his illness would lead to the most celebrated sporting pastime ever manifest: the safari. The origins of the word stem from Arabic terms—the verb *safara* meaning to "unveil" in classic Arabic and the noun *safariya*, to "expedition or journey." The combination of the two, then, became *safari*. European hunters adopted the term in the late 19th century when they began to hunt the Arab strongholds of East Africa. No word in the hunters' lexicon stirs more lust for adventure: safari is the one term more than any other that best embodies the spirit that defines what it is to be a hunter—bold, independent, rugged, and pioneering.

Although Cornwallis was among the first to venture to Africa for the express purpose of hunting, William Burchell's 1811 foray into the interior of the continent (nearly to present-day Botswana) was the first such expedition by a white man. Burchell's classic work, *Travels in the Interior of Southern Africa*, was subsequently published in 1822. Anyone who has read about or traveled to Africa recognizes the name Burchell because the continent is rife with scores of flora and fauna named after the intrepid botanist.

While the heyday of the African big-game safari began in the mid-19th century and lasted until about World War II, the best of the bird-hunting safaris may yet lie ahead. Even during Teddy Roosevelt's famous 1909 safari, the retired president made time for bustard and wood stork shooting. While neither bird represented what most contemporary wingshooters view as classic bird-hunting fare, the hunts did serve to make adventuresome sports aware that there was more to the African safari experience than chasing the continent's megafauna with double rifles.

The popularity of the wingshooting safari began to rise as growing legions of African big-game hunters paused between lion and buffalo stalking to enjoy the wealth of game birds found throughout much of the continent. These wingshooting interludes began to pique the curiosity of enterprising professional hunters who were looking to take advantage of abundant game bird resources and a growing interest by foreign hunters in wingshooting.

In the early 1970s, the legendary tandem of Bing Crosby and Phil Harris traveled with the crew of the widely popular *The American Sportsman* television series to enjoy sandgrouse gunning near Lake Tanganyika. For millions of American hunters like myself, it was the first time most of us had ever even heard of a bird called a sandgrouse. Couple the sporty nature of the bird with the magnetism of the two celebrity icons enjoying the shooting and you have a stellar introduction to African wingshooting.

Today, scores of qualified African outfitters cater exclusively to bird shooters. Dozens of upland game birds can be found across much of Africa—including numerous species of the partridge-like francolin. Of all the driven-bird shooting available across the globe, none is more intriguing and resplendent with anticipation than driven guinea fowl. When beaters enter cover in Africa, a whole host of birds and mammals may exit—not the least of which might be the dangerous game for which the continent is so famous. Waterfowl—including the prehis-

toric-looking spurwing goose—offer visiting duck and goose hunters varied gunning over rivers, sloughs, and fields.

No matter what your wingshooting fancy, no place rivals Africa for her mixture of landscapes, big-game viewing or hunting, and wingshooting. It offers, indeed, the world's wildest shotgunning.

Helmeted guinea fowl (Numida meleagris).

CHAPTER 6

An African Journey
~ ZIMBABWE ~

I t starts as a simple bird hunt. We stop the Land Rover and uncase our guns, and soon a trio of pointers is kicking up dust contrails ahead of us. Before the hunt has a chance to develop any rhythm, however, one of the trackers brings word that there's a herd of 14 elephants just ahead. Dung piles the size of large anthills and a trail of broken tree branches litter their path; an elephant is something of a tornado with feet. An entire cast of lesser mammals, however, depends on elephants to push, pull, yank, or knock food within reach.

Professional hunter Steve Seward swaps his 12 bore for a .416 Winchester bolt-action rifle—a gun whose lipstick-sized, 300-grain cartridges are good medicine for unruly pachyderms. Our hunt continues, but the character of it changes. I spend more time scanning the acacias ahead than I do watching the dogs for bird work. We are hunting in the 1.2 million-acre Savé Conservancy in southern Zimbabwe, and the elephants come from Gonarezhou National Park near the Mozambique border. It's there that guerrilla troops armed with Soviet-supplied AK-47s poached them for

Following a morning of driven guinea fowl shooting, our party returns to the comforts of a lodge within Zimbabwe's 1.2 million-acre Savé Conservancy.

In Africa you are never far from surreal vistas. Hunting in the shadow of elephants adds an exotic flare to bird shooting.

A covey of guineas is about to meet professional hunter Steve Seward and his 12 gauge. The chicken-sized birds can absorb several pellets without succumbing.

meat and ivory. The elephants haven't forgotten and are noticeably more aggressive than tuskers from more protected regions.

Like the elephant, the black rhino—one of the most endangered beasts on the planet—is also suffering at the hands of poachers ravaging the underfunded national parks. In a historic response, the Zimbabwe government moved the animals to more secure private holdings such as Savé—a place where each rhino is followed by an armed game scout. It was a move that undoubtedly prevented the extirpation of the nation's rhinos.

Seward blows his dog whistle regularly, announcing our presence in advance to give the elephants ample time to stay well ahead of us. As we fixate on pachyderms, Swempie—a liver-and-white pointer whose name translates to *cocqui francolin* in the Shona language—makes game. Another pointer, Rigby, follows suit, cornering a small covey of Shelly's francolin under the tentacle-like branches of a young (less than 200 years old) baobab tree. I miss an easy straightaway but connect on a cock partially shielded behind cover. The dogs introduce us to three more coveys as we complete our circle back to the Rover . . . elephant free.

The next morning begins at sunrise when we strike off in the Rover in search of guineas, that most elusive of African game birds. The

A pair of guineas are soon to fall to Steve Seward's double-gun. Note the shot charge on its way to the first bird.

Above: A pet eland wanders in to inspect the remnants of one of its distant relatives. Dining on game cooked over an open fire is one of the great pleasures of the African safari.

Right: A surprising number of quality pointing dogs are found throughout southern Africa, providing spectacular rough shooting for a variety of francolin species as well as guinea fowl.

Opposite page: Veteran African wingshooter Tina Dunlap connects with a Swainson's francolin in southern Zimbabwe. The chukar-sized birds are explosive flushers and are as splendid on the table as they are over a point.

birds are sometimes found in coveys numbering in the hundreds. Seward's notion is to surround the birds with a crew of beaters and drive them toward a line of guns. Orchestrating a successful drive is an art form on the order of herding tumbleweeds in a gale. When

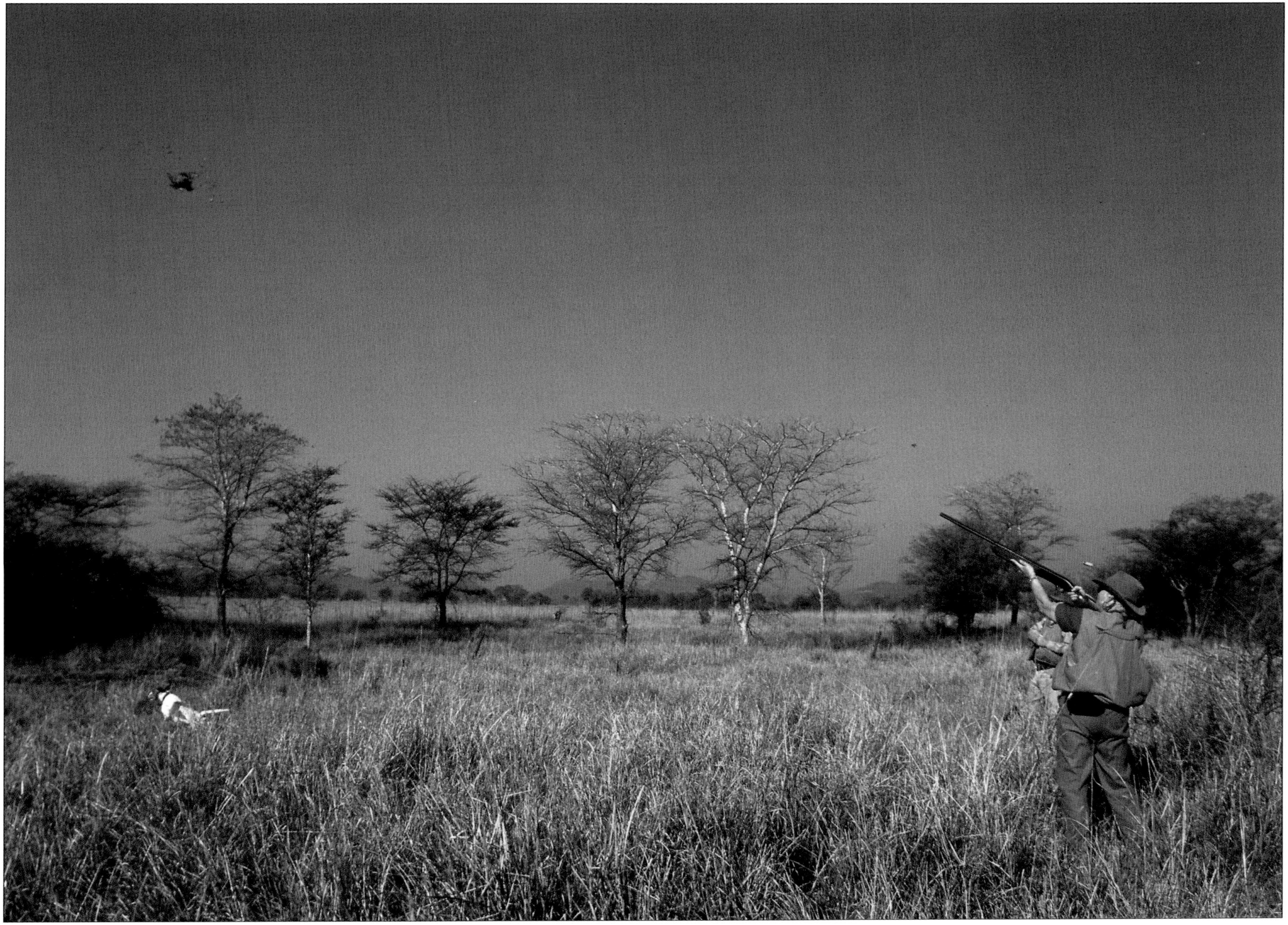

AN AFRICAN JOURNEY (ZIMBABWE)

Sometimes it's difficult to see the guineas for the trees. These bombers of the bushveld are spectacular game birds that fly deceptively fast.

it works, however, the wingshooting world knows no moment so sweet. An airborne guinea is an imposing target, black bombers that deceive even veterans of driven shoots on the grouse moors of Scotland.

Our Rover is followed by a pickup transporting a crew of beaters, pointers, and Labs. As we locate a flock of guineas in the distance, the driving team is deployed by Seward, who instructs them authoritatively, the way he might have his elite SAS unit during the bloody Rhodesian war. The contingent loops behind the birds as the fowl scratch and peck through the veld in search of seeds and insects, yet oblivious to our presence. Seward, meanwhile, leads his line of guns consisting of John and Tina Dunlap, a California couple making their ninth trip to Zimbabwe to get their annual fix of driven-guinea shooting.

Once in position, Seward radios the beaters to begin the procession. A driven guinea hunt is most often a feast or famine affair, and the task sometimes seems as practical as shoveling water. Nevertheless, enough such maneuvers succeed to command repeat attempts. In the distance—perhaps 100 yards ahead—the clicking chatter of guineas builds in a crescendo, letting us know that they have tweaked to the beaters and are about to fly . . . the question is, which way? The covey launches in near unison, a din of wingbeats and calling. In

Victoria Falls is perhaps the most dramatic waterfall in the world and is a must-see for any visitor to Zimbabwe.

moments, the main aggregation of the flock passes down the line to my left, but a trio of birds splits the difference between Tina and me. I focus on the closest of the lot and fold it with my second barrel. A flurry of shots ring from the end of the line where Tina's husband intercepts a brace of the escaping birds.

One of the beauties of driven shooting in Africa is that one never knows for sure what might flush. A family of warthogs, their tails as erect as antennas, shuffles past me 15 yards to the south. A francolin drive in Botswana's Okavango Delta once produced an old bull Cape buffalo, a moment of terror followed by elation as the beast chose a course perpendicular to me. "Nothing so exhilarating as to be shot at and missed," once opined Winston Churchill.

POINT OF NO RETURN

We return to Seward's tented safari camp near Chinoi, a small but bustling hamlet some two hours north of the capital of Harare. Southern Africa is littered with lodges these days—places with all the convenience of the Ritz. The safari experience, however, is about tent caps with open fires and warthog on the grill and enough elixir to erode your ties—if even for one night—to the industrial world. It's about stepping back in time to enjoy a simple existence on the land, and by the land.

Above: Scouting a field for guineas, a pair of professional hunters make a plan to encircle the birds and drive them toward a line of guns that will be hidden in nearby bush.

Right: This is what a guinea fowl looks like standing still. They don't make film fast enough to capture the bird's speed while running.

En route, talk turns to that of Africa's many fascinating and dangerous animals. "The most dangerous beast in Africa," says Seward wryly, "is the bloody donkey. It's a real surprise when you find one in your headlights as you round a bend at night."

A professional hunter must be many things: part comedian to know when to lift his client's spirits, part naturalist to answer the myriad questions every bloke passing through his camp feels obliged to ask, part predator to seek out game stealthily, part mechanic to fix the inevitable problems brought about by the rigors of the safari trail, part gunsmith to make sure a hunter's guns—an insurance policy and

Above: White-faced whistling ducks are stunningly beautiful fowl that readily decoy to even simple spreads.

Left: This Egyptian goose is perched high atop a dead tree bordering a Zimbabwe reservoir that provided memorable duck and goose gunning.

grocery store rolled into one—are working at all times, and, finally, part tour guide to share the enthusiasm of a first-time traveler to the Dark Continent. Seward is all that and more.

We turn our attention from the uplands to the nation's wetlands, for southern Africa's bird wealth includes myriad wildfowl species. The comb duck, a peculiar goose-sized bird with a silver-dollar-sized fleshy knob above its bill, is a mainstay of what few waterfowlers exist in Zimbabwe. White-faced whistling ducks, red-billed teal, and Egyptian geese make up the majority of birds we'll encounter.

Our host for an afternoon hunt is David Penny, a young tobacco farmer whose immac-

Egyptian geese congregate in a shallow marsh near Chinoi, Zimbabwe. The birds are roughly the dimension of a midsized Canada goose and possess a raucus call in flight.

ulate plantation-style estate hints that there are riches found in the green leaves. His newly constructed 300-acre impoundment, one of several such wetlands on his property, is a favorite destination for thousands of visiting ducks and geese. His passion for retriever training proves useful as we employ one of his pupils to recover birds. Seward's skilled Lab completes the retriever tandem that would be tested this day.

The impoundment resembles a small California lake, surrounded by arid landscape. A series of trees, killed by the floodwaters stored by the dam, provide wooden perches for both the whistling ducks and Egyptian geese. Our blind sits starkly along the bank of the reservoir, and I convince my host that a decoy spread would be the *piece de resistance* for the birds. Lacking a ready supply of faux birds, we improvise by tying strings weighted by rocks to 20 white milk cartons. Judging from the looks shot back and forth between Seward and Penny, the duo is more than a little skeptical of my recommendation. As gracious hosts, however. they humor my request—if for no other reason than to be able to tell a Yank, if the tactic proves unsuccessful, "I told you so!"

Like sea ducks duped by black jugs tied to a rope, the African fowl pitch to the opening left between two circles of containers as if coming to newly painted Mason decoys. Vindication

comes with each approaching flight, and the Africans taste the virtues of shooting over decoys. A modified wigeon call completes the adaptations—American waterfowlers are nothing if not bound by tradition—a fact two Africans come to understand, if not appreciate.

A WING AND A PRAYER

Running out of cash and desperate to carve out a life together, Trevor and Collette Comins struggled to find a way to extract a living from the South African landscape. Only after exhausting conventional employment, the couple came upon the idea of opening a bird-hunting operation. The idea was received with laughter and no small amount of skepticism among the country's big-game outfitters. Some 20 years later, however, thanks to the success of the Comins' wingshooting safaris, many of South Africa's big-game outfitters are dovetailing bird hunting with their commercial big-game hunting ventures.

As Trevor will tell it, though, it takes years of experience to get it right, and his education came through trial and error and firsthand exposure to international wingshooters. "It's got to be right," he says, "or they just won't come back."

It's that approach to his business that has brought him a steady cadre of repeat clients—the testimonial for any hunting outfitter. It is the nation's abundance of birds, coupled with Trevor's careful stewardship of that resource, that has allowed him to grow his list of guests.

His Tendele Lodge sits in the Montana-like countryside of eastern South Africa, an area once dominated by the kingdom of Shaka

Zula, the greatest warrior the Zulu nation has ever known. It's an area where both upland birds (predominantly Swainson's and Shelly's francolin) and waterfowl (yellow-billed ducks, red-billed teal, and Egyptian geese) are found. The marquee attractions, however, are guinea fowl and spurwing geese, black and white birds that resemble a hybrid of a muscovy duck and a black swan. While the guineas are driven, the spurwing decoy like the rest of South Africa's waterfowl—providing a mixed assortment of ducks and geese on several of Trevor's many hunting venues.

With homemade spurwing silhouettes staked along the edge of a 5-acre slough, I greet dawn with the expectation that the monstrous birds will be coming soon. As is usually the case when hunting with Trevor, the birds arrive as if on cue. For such ponderous birds, they utter a remarkably subtle hissing noise—enough to set the hair on the nape of any waterfowler's neck on end with anticipation. A dozen birds glide through the gray light of a cloud-covered morning, their wingtips tapping

the air currents ever so slightly. In the slow motion of the shooting sequence, I swing the gun ahead of the lead bird and merely send the flock into aerial contortions in that awkward moment when the birds first discern that something is dreadfully wrong with their descent. The second barrel betrays me as well—a remarkable phenomenon given the amount of air space above my blind covered by birds. It wouldn't have been so humiliating save for the fact that there are witnesses to the travesty . . . witnesses with long memories.

As fortune has it, there are soon opportunities for redemption as myriad small flocks of whistling ducks, red-billed teal, Egyptian geese, and more spurwings arrive from a nearby reservoir. Several catch the ire of my 12 bore, later to become the staple of an equally memorable dinner at Tendele. Trevor's daughter, Camilla, is a *chef de parte*, which is to say she is something of an alchemist, transforming the treasures of the field into riches on the table. It is all part of the African safari tradition, a hunting event unrivaled in the annals of sport.

Helmeted guinea fowl (Numida meleagris).

CHAPTER 7

Africa's Feathered Treasures

⌒ SOUTH AFRICA ⌒

he beast is dead, but that's when it becomes dangerous. Forty yards in the sky, the 22-pound spurwinged goose plummets toward my blind. When calculating the lead on the bird, I neglect to consider what might happen if my shot is indeed successful. The head-

lines fly through my mind: "Kamikaze Goose KOs Nimrod," or "Bird Brains Hunter." The thought of leaping into the water to miss the plumed mete-orite flits through my thoughts until I remember the crocodile that patrolled past my hide only a few minutes earlier. During my indecision, the bird smacks the earth behind me with a bone-crushing thud. Of the world's sporting birds, the spurwing comes the closest to being dangerous game. "They're the Cape buffalo of African birds," jokes Trevor Comins, a professional hunter who's logged countless miles into the South African bush.

Spurwings are seemingly a throwback to the Mesozoic era, a bird one might imagine as the successor to the pterodactyl. The most distinguishing

The Vryheid area of South Africa is reminiscent of the eastern Montana plains. Small livestock reservoirs throughout the agricultural region provide ideal venues in which to hunt both ducks and geese.

known simply as Zululand, a name that rolls easily off the tongue.

The open banks along the watercourse are preferred rest areas for spurwings, and Trevor arranges a few dozen homemade silhouette spurwing decoys along with several Canada goose shells he's imported from America. The region's other geese, the Egyptian variety, are roughly the dimensions of a small- to medium-sized honker and readily decoy to the Canada dupes.

"Mark right!" shouts Trevor from the cover behind us. A flock of white-faced whistling ducks approaches, announcing their presence with their distinctive three-note whistle. This handsome duck is found in both South America and Africa, inhabiting tropical lowlands across the eastern half of the Dark Continent. The long form of the birds in flight and their peculiar white faces make them easy to identify. Richard plucks one of the birds from the flock before they flare to other waters.

Yellow-billed ducks and red-billed teal share the skies with the geese and whistling ducks, diversifying our bag. Bird boys use rowboats to fetch the fallen ducks and geese, for the waters teem with crocs that have a penchant for being hard-mouthed when it comes to Labs. Trevor's crew is delayed in reaching one of the fall-

Yellow-billed duck (Anas undulata).

feature of the spurwing is its sheer size—it is the largest goose on the planet. With a wingspan over 6 feet, the spurwing appears to lumber into the sky, and, once airborne, it's about as maneuverable as the *Spruce Goose.* But spurwings are tough. Ugly too. They're the linebackers of the avian world—one part tenacity, two parts' attitude. I share a blind with Mississippian Bob Cooke, and farther down the bank of the river rest Richard and Marci Welker, a Michigan couple enjoying their first African wingshooting safari. Our blinds stand some 20 miles from the Indian Ocean, along a river channel lined with open dirt banks framed by towering canes. We are in South Africa's KwaZulu Natal region, a bird-rich area probably best en spurwings, and a hungry croc makes certain the bird doesn't go to waste. It isn't clear what it takes to be drafted for retrieving duty here, but it is likely a profession that doesn't come with a pension.

The crocs aren't alone in the river, however, as the ballooning faces of hippos periodically surface out of the water. At first glance, they are seemingly sublime plant eaters whose doughboy appearance belies their malevolent nature. "They've killed more people in Africa than any other animal," says Trevor with a watchful eye and a tone of mistrust in his voice. This is an amazing fact when one thinks of the considerable cast of African beasts whose menus have included *Homo sapiens*.

"Mark right!" shouts Trevor, ending our brief conversation the moment he spies a pair of Egyptian geese sailing toward us. The pair passes wide of Richard's blind but swing overhead. It is an easy double. It should have been an easy double. I still can't believe that I didn't bust a feather. "Mr. Dorsey, do you need some toilet paper?" queries Trevor with a smirk growing wide across his face.

"For what?" I ask, willfully stepping into his trap.

Red-billed duck (Anas erythrorhyncha).

"To wipe the dirt out of your eyes so you can see to shoot." Laughter erupts from the blinds, and Trevor translates the joke to his Zulu staff members, who have the same reaction. Trevor is part field general, part comedian; is fluent in Zulu, Afrikaans, and English; and speaks enough German to get into trouble. He grew up with the Zulus, his father once recruiting them to work in the country's rich diamond mines. His résumé includes tenure as a game warden who helped found the Itala Nature Reserve in the former Zululand. He and his wife, Colette, are skilled hosts, quickly acclimating their guests to the casual lifestyle of an African wingshooting safari.

Above: A Swainson's francolin momentarily escapes the wrath of hunters near Vryheid, South Africa.

Right: A spurwing goose for the pot. These are the largest geese on the planet, weighing upwards of 20 pounds.

THE FABLED TENDELE LODGE

The stone walls and floors of Tendele—Zulu for "partridge"—and the many mounts of African game birds that adorn the great receiving room are instantly welcoming to wingshooters who follow the rumors of memorable bird hunting emanating from South Africa. Hardwood tables and bookshelves replete with scores of sporting titles add to the atmosphere. A small sign behind the bar sets the tone of the experience, "Relax, you're on safari." Underfoot are zebra

Tendele Lodge near Vryheid, South Africa, is among the oldest wingshooting lodges in all of Africa. From here, hunters can enjoy both upland bird and waterfowl hunting.

rugs, and in the corner sits a piano in case any guest is moved to music by the combination of ample wine and the spirit of adventure that accompanies any worthwhile safari.

Tendele was built in 1948 by former Italian prisoners of war who remained in South Africa after World War II. It's located near the predominantly Afrikaans community of Vryheid in South Africa's Natal Province, a region blessed with abundant wingshooting opportunities. Our introduction to the area's waterfowling comes early the first morning of the sojourn. We arrive at our blinds before dawn. Sturdy hides with wooden frames and cane sides complete with cushioned seats sit at the

confluence of a small stream that feeds into a 120-acre reservoir.

First in are the darting forms of the red-billed teal, as challenging a target as their brethren the world over. Shoot once and the birds immediately flare skyward with astonishing speed. Waves of the mallard-sized yellow-billed ducks and white-faced whistling ducks soon follow,

Returning after a morning of duck and goose gunning, a hunter walks past birds that have been hand selected for the evening dinner of duck a l'Orange.

Duck hunting near the Blood River is among the most memorable waterfowling found anywhere. Here, host Trevor Comins instructs one of his gunners on the finer points of teal shooting.

enchanting the African dawn with their presence. Richard is the first to intercept one of the teal; Bob and I follow soon with hits of our own. Several flocks of the birds appear like necklaces on the horizon, their dark forms obvious against the amber sunrise. The flurry of whistling wings lasts for more than an hour, giving each of us ample opportunities to miss.

We return to the lodge and are greeted by Trevor's daughter, Camilla. She and Colette have been busy preparing brunch: eggs Benedict, toast from homemade bread, fresh fruit, and yogurt. "I'm not sure if our hunters keep coming back for the food or for the hunting," says Trevor, rubbing his soon-to-be-expanding stomach.

Above: Inside South Africa's famed Tendele Lodge hunters relive the day's shoot as countless others have done for the past quarter century.

Right: The morning's take of spurwings, white-faced whistling ducks, and yellow-billed ducks in Zululand.

Opposite page: Comins' team makes short work of retrieves while aboard the small craft floating in the croc-infested waters found in Zululand. (Photo by R. Valentine Atkinson.)

The variety of game bird species in South Africa is perhaps unmatched anywhere in the world. In addition to many kinds of waterfowl, some 12 species of francolin—upland birds ranging in size from partridges to pheasants—and many species of doves, pigeons, and quail are also found here. "The key to maintaining quality waterfowling," says Trevor, "is to provide plenty of rest areas for the ducks. You mustn't overshoot your birds."

He hunts an area some 500,000 acres

A pack of hippos stage just downriver from our decoys in Zululand. While the animals appear placid enough, they are among the most dangerous beasts in Africa.

in size, developing cooperative arrangements with farmers who sell him hunting rights. "When the landowners see financial value in the game," he says, "they begin to manage the land to accommodate more wildlife." Such a theme is becoming even more prevalent across Africa and the rest of the world: wildlife that pays, stays.

Trevor has also secured many parcels resplendent in francolin reserves. The Swainson's francolin, a bird roughly the size of a hen pheasant and equally as presentable as table fare, is the most prevalent in the region. We set out behind Vondwe, a two-year-old German shorthaired pointer. "*Vondwe* is Zulu for 'cane rat,'" says Trevor. "We call him that because he's so ugly." There's nothing so beautiful, however, as a precision-pointing dog sifting the air currents until freezing stoically on point. Vondwe's methodical style makes him easy to follow, and he provides nearly 20 birds over point. Each of us rotates shooting chances, captivated by the mesmerizing dog work and feathers-in-your-face flushes.

DROVES OF GUINEA FOWL

Driving guinea fowl can be like lassoing smoke. Although there is no shortage of the birds on the plains of southern Africa,

they seem more closely related to cheetahs than to game birds. In a 100-yard dash between a guinea fowl and a pheasant, put your money on the guinea and don't worry about spotting the rooster 30 yards.

After two frustrating attempts to corral flocks of hundreds of guineas, Trevor refuses to concede to the beasts. Having developed something of a vendetta against the birds, he formulates a strategy to trap them on the slope of a coulee dotted with acacias, the thorned trees that are the hallmark of the African bushveld.

With gunners positioned in a line stretching the length of the slope, Trevor leads his team of a dozen beaters in a quick march to surround the birds that we watch slip into the grass and acacia cover. In moments, Trevor sounds his horn, signaling that the first birds of the drive are airborne

White-faced whistling ducks circle my blind while I'm tucked along the edge of a lagoon in Zululand.

and heading for the guns. This time the ambush works. Guns pop below the hill as Bob and Richard bring several of the helmeted guinea fowl to earth. Their name is derived from the helmet shape of their plated heads, though it could just as easily come from the relative toughness of the birds.

Trevor's horn soon becomes a serenade as the mother lode of the birds takes flight like a guinea migration and, in the distance, he conducts his orchestra of beaters by waving his flushing stick hither and yon. A flock of 20 guineas swing overhead, intermittently flapping and gliding as they seek to reach distant covers. I pull one of the birds down, tipping it with the first barrel and finishing the job with the second. I quickly reload as more birds approach. This time a double falls to my reports, and in the distance Bob and Richard busily intercept birds of their own.

Guinea fowl shooting doesn't enjoy the esteem of driven grouse on the Scottish moors, but that could be because those who have seen the veld come alive with the sight of hundreds of airborne guineas aren't telling anyone. Whether for waterfowl, francolin, doves, pigeons, or driven guineas, the new South Africa remains the wingshooting world's best-kept secret.

Greywing francolin (Francolinus africanus).

CHAPTER 8

Flying Times in the Cape
SOUTH AFRICA

e sit, out of breath and speechless, in the front row of a geologic theater. Below the mountainous bluffs on which we rest stretches the rest of Africa, the sometimes sorrowful and often compelling continent that she is. To look out is to wonder what the future might hold, to hope that we might one day return to the same place, if never the same moment in time.

I can only wonder what Robin Halse is thinking as he rests his side-by-side across his lap, lights his pipe, and stares into the abyss below. He has been to these bluffs a thousand times before, but the place, like a well-rested whiskey, begs to be savored. His ancestors left England some 130 years ago during the depression that followed the Napoleonic wars to settle this land that lies in the shadow of Mount Andriesberg, located in the Cape Province of northeast South Africa.

His family has been stalking the same greywing francolin coveys for generations, always mindful to leave plenty of birds to seed the future for aspiring wingshots. Greywings are but one of many francolin varieties to inhabit the country, and there are scores of quail, dove, and guinea fowl species to confound gun-

Robin Halse and Roddy Watson crest a ridge on Carnarvon Estates, a 20,000-acre greywing paradise located in South Africa's Cape Province.

South African shelduck (Tadorna cana).

ners here as well. But it is the greywings on Halse's 20,000-acre Carnarvon Estate that have catapulted wingshooting to legendary status. These birds are similar in size and color to Hungarian partridges and even emit the same sort of frog-choking squawk when they are forced to take flight under protest.

It is a sound—like a Pavlovian response—that I quickly associate with pleasant times. As the sun sets over the arid mountains, we reverse our afternoon's course and return to Robin's Land Rover—the iron beast that has endured years of rock climbing and, God willing, would make it down the mountain to Black Eagle Lodge one more time. That seems especially important as Robin's wife, Berta, is preparing a lavish meal—an event for which not even the greywings take precedence. Joining us are Roddy Watson and Grania Williams, a couple newly arrived from England, where Roddy is the proprietor of the prestigious West London Shooting School.

Sitting down to feast after a rigorous day of greywing chasing in the mountains seems an especially fitting way to spend life. Indeed, it's good work when you can find it. The evening starts, as do most here, with a glass of port followed by one or two of the Cape's vintage wines. We then spill into the dining area of the lodge, where Berta unveils a succulent roast of lamb, the wafts from which had primed our

taste buds for half an hour. The flavor lives up to the aroma, a dining experience remembered for its spirit as well as succulence.

Sufficiently stuffed and pleasantly tired, we stoke the fire and melt into the soft chairs that form a semicircle around the blaze. At the foot of the fire rests three foot-sore and hunt-weary pointers—Tessa, Cyclops, and Wally—a trio of dogs that know much about greywings

and are happy to share their knowledge with visiting hunters. They are the most amiable pointers I've yet to encounter, sporting disarming tailwags and a general affection for people that suggest they know life as a Halse dog is indeed something to celebrate.

While all three pointers display an abundance of hunting wizardry, I make sure I never stray too far from Tessa, the 12-year-old sage

The rocky bluffs of the eastern Cape provide ideal habitat for greywing francolin, the sportiest of South Africa's many francolin species. They are covey risers that use the region's ever-present wind and angles to their advantage.

Above: Inside the main house at Carnarvon—even Halse's pointers are afforded a chance to curl up by the fire.

Right: Greywings often sit well for a point, and the dogs found at Carnarvon are especially skilled at finding these diminutive game birds.

of the lot. She moves with economy through the pakkan shrubs, never wasting the effort that younger dogs are often wont to do. Having left an aging setter at home, I adopt Tessa as my personal bird dog for the trip. We log countless miles over the rugged terrain, and she ceaselessly amazes me with her durability and pointing prowess. Unable to keep pace with the younger Cyclops and Wally, Tessa becomes a specialist at finding birds the others miss. It is an endearing quality for which I become particularly fond.

Only a few paces down the edge of a bluff, Cyclops rounds a boulder and stiffens with the scent of a lone greywing flying through his brain. This time there is synergy between Robin's double-triggered BSA and me. I tap the first hammer, sending the bird spinning to earth without the need for a second shot. That is particularly important as a double-triggered shotgun in my hands is, well, effectively a single-shot gun (or a conservation tool).

It is with a great deal of admiration and a bit of envy that I watch Roddy and Robin work their double triggers without the where-the-hell-is-that-second-trigger that is the hallmark of my experiences with the contraptions. At the outset of the hunt, it seems a keen idea to indulge myself in the South African wingshooting traditions—double-triggers and all—but by the end of the experience I long for one of my single-selectives back home the way one craves a trained dog after hunting with an unruly pup. I have 10 days of big-game hunting awaiting me at the end of the bird-hunting junket, so my gun case is filled with two rifles but no shotgun—a mistake I vow never to repeat.

My longing for a single-triggered gun intensifies as we embark on a driven guinea fowl shoot. These are helmeted guinea fowl, one of two species of guineas found in South Africa. Judging from the number of birds that escape my wrath, however, they are also armored guinea fowl. The birds are adept at scrambling on foot to elude predators, which is why they are often disagreeable when it comes to taking

Above top: Sarah Halse is both a skilled farmhand and dog handler, two skills that are especially valuable at Carnarvon.

Above bottom: Halse's cabins built in the mountains above Carnarvon are located amid spectacular vistas and some of the region's best greywing francolin hunting.

flight. Robin's solution is simple, however. The gunners form a line across the grass expanse of the gentle fields found on the estate's lowlands. Perhaps a quarter mile away, professional hunter Kent Olivier—one of only a few black professional hunters in South Africa—leads a crew of drivers in a line toward us.

Countless numbers of the avian bombers sail over my gun, as though they sense a weakness in our defensive strategy. They have. I intercept but a few of the many birds that fly over my gun, for the most part feeling like an ambassador who has betrayed his flag.

By the last day of the greywing odyssey, the BSA grows workable in my grasp, if not comfortable. We begin the morning with a family breakfast that includes the company of two of Robin's three daughters, Sarah and Ann, and Ann's husband, Sean. Hunters here become honorary members of the family, and once you get to know this clan you'll begin to realize what a distinction that is.

This is a typical breakfast, which is to say it is easy to eat oneself out of condition to hunt. We begin with porridge, toast, and fruit—alone, enough calories to sustain a sumo. Home-cured ham, bacon, and eggs follow with fresh-squeezed juice from Cape-grown oranges and homemade preserves and hand-churned butter. Cholesterol counters and diet watchers need not apply.

A brace of greywings before they became appetizers. The succulent, white-meated birds taste much like quail.

Hiking the wind-swept hills surrounding the farm is rigorous activity, so it is easy to burn added calories in the process. There is something of a primordial satisfaction in hunting hard and gorging oneself. It's a simple existence with a clear purpose—to have fun. It is such days when it is easy to forget the hectic confusion of a demanding office—the very same days we remember with special reverence when the hassles of civilization hang around us like a sticky web from which escape is cumbersome.

After ruminating over the heaping breakfast, we pause for brief solace next to the fire before facing the howling winds awaiting outside. The pointers climb over one another like blind pups in search of a spare nipple as they attempt to inch closer to the fire. Robin, meanwhile, leans back, strikes a match, and lights his pipe—puffing the tobacco to life as a plume of smoke hangs over his head ghostlike, highlighted by the morning sun shining through the panes behind him.

Robin often follows his meals with a smoke; it is a small part of the order and cadence that is so much a part of his existence. There is existing, and then there is being alive, a distinction not lost on the elder Halse. Hunts are never rushed here, and conversations, if postponed, are always finished. He has an innate sense of making time for items of signif-

icance, and by making time for them, he alerts one always to what is important to him. The ritual of the hunt at Carnarvon is always paramount on his list of worthwhile events.

His passion for the affair is obvious from his first steps into the rocky hillsides. The wind threatens to blow us back down the hill as we stride for the downwind side—the place, we concurred, that is most likely to harbor the greywing coveys of the area. Shortly after reaching the ridge crest, Cyclops locates a pair of birds below Robin and Roddy. In the wind, I can hear nothing of the exchange between the

two hunters, and the shots fired in the gusts at the departing birds could have been a mile away if the sound were any indication—instead of merely 70 yards to the west. Roddy tumbles the two birds despite the tailwind that blows them quickly downrange like leaves in a gale.

By the time we return home from the afternoon hunt, Berta's kitchen permeates with the aroma of roast guinea fowl, potatoes, carrots, and freshly made ice cream. Life cannot be considered complete until you've sampled a dish of Berta's ice cream with a spoonful of chocolate syrup dripped zebra-like over

Shelduck (Tadorna tadorna).

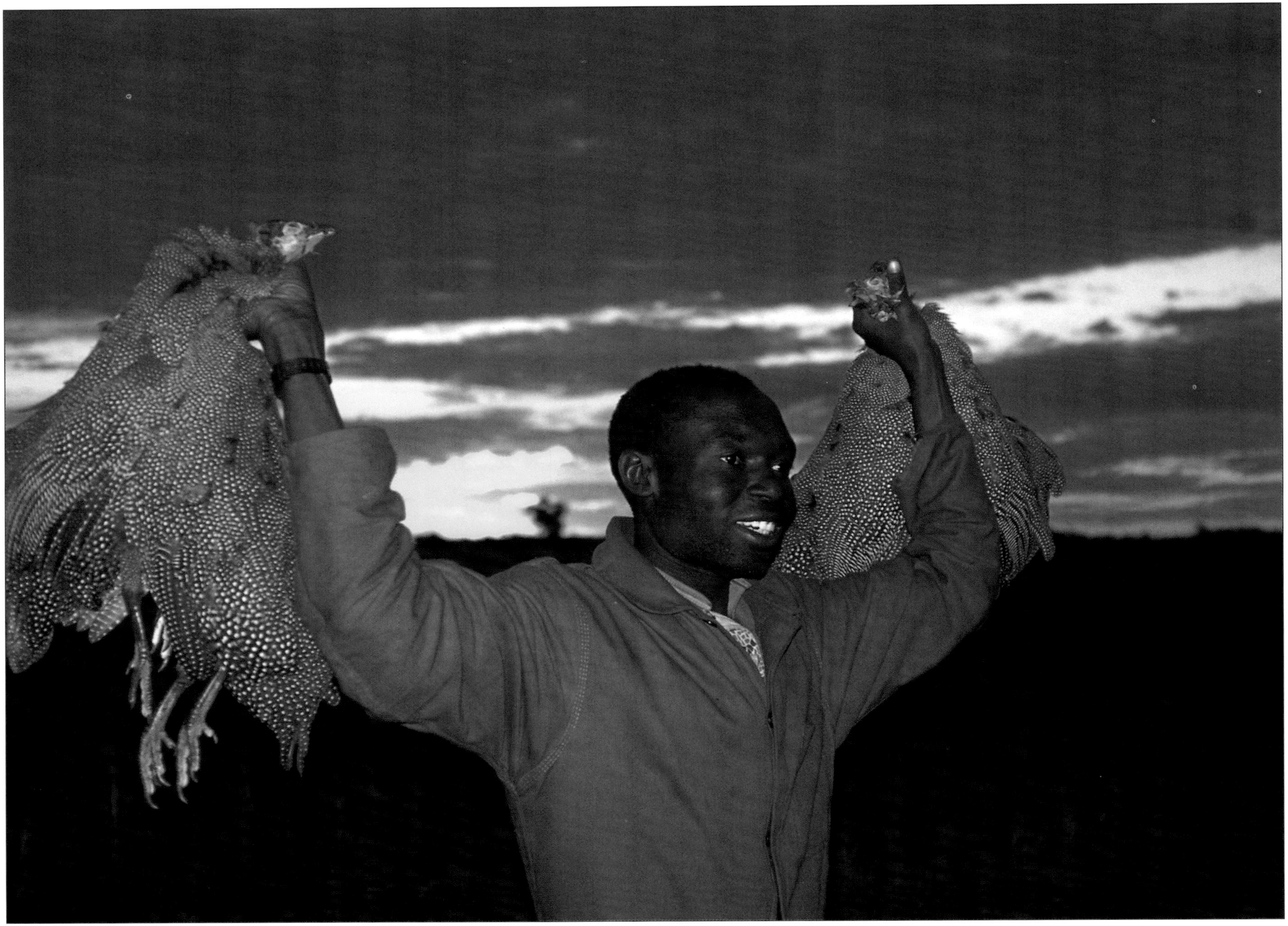

Above: In addition to greywing, Carnarvon holds large numbers of guinea fowl. Drives frequently produce large flocks of the chicken-sized birds.

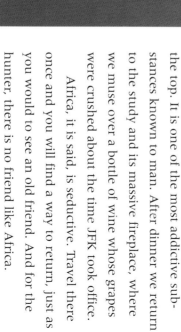

Left: Seemingly docile birds while drinking at a water-hole, guinea fowl are capable of outdistancing the fastest human sprinters without ever leaving the ground.

Opposite page: Despite their tenacity, guinea fowl can be effectively driven to a line of guns—so long as the guns slip into position without being detected by the birds.

the top. It is one of the most addictive sub-stances known to man. After dinner we return to the study and its massive fireplace, where we muse over a bottle of wine whose grapes were crushed about the time JFK took office.

Africa, it is said, is seductive. Travel there once and you will find a way to return, just as you would to see an old friend. And for the hunter, there is no friend like Africa.

Crested francolin (Francolinus sephaena).

CHAPTER 9

Moor and Better Wingshooting
∽ SOUTH AFRICA ∽

erhaps the greatest of all personal ironies is that a life is a mystery that can never be solved by the person living it. The best we can hope for are a few revelations along the way. For Alistair McLean, the fiftysomething son of a Scottish gamekeeper who could only dream of a better existence for his son, there was no way of knowing how far his life's journey would take him. When he was but a young boy, his family immigrated to South Africa, where the clan would labor to survive. Alistair's trek of 40 years would see him reach a new position in life, one that allows him to appreciate the sacrifices he saw his father make to give him the gift of hope. It is only after his father's death that Alistair has grown closest to his father, as the decisions that once seemed a riddle now have meaning.

Many ponds and tanks throughout South Africa support sandgrouse populations.

Alistair and I are standing atop the Drakensberg Mountains of South Africa—peaks just tall enough that, if a person has the right perspective, he might even see

the moors of Scotland and a tired gamekeeper forever walking the slopes for birds. A man's view of his destiny is never clearer than when he's looking back—perhaps perched high on a mountain, far away from the haze of modern life. It is the picture of his Scottish roots that is frozen in Alistair's mind, and the memory of his father revisits him as we pause for a moment of rest. A lifetime of hard work, business acumen, and a healthy dose of good for-

Above: A guinea fowl-francolin mixed bag on the Springbok Flats. There's no shortage of game-bird hunting opportunities across South Africa.

Right: South African professional dog trainer Dave Fowler isn't ready for a surprise flush by the second of two Swainson's francolin.

Opposite page: In heavy cover, Swainson's will often sit tight for a pointing dog. Rough-shooting the birds, thus, is great sport—much like early-season pheasant hunting on the Dakota prairie.

tune now make possible his return journeys to the Scottish game fields where he renews his affair with red grouse and personal history each September. In his mind's eye, it is Alistair's father who is pushing the birds to him . . . across a generation. Add heather to the slopes of the Drakensbergs and you could be transported to the British Isles in spirit, if not in person—especially if part of you never left.

South Africa, however, is now Alistair's home in every sense and will be the place where his mystery will be solved. The question that will haunt Alistair is whether his own son will one day come to understand the shoulders upon which he is standing. Alistair has poured tears and toil into South Africa, weaving his family into the fabric of the nation. Unlike so many of his white countrymen who fear what

Alistair McLean's stunning lodge located north of Jo'burg is positioned amid some of the nation's finest upland game bird hunting.

In the Kalahari region of South Africa, gunners can enjoy the country's best sandgrouse gunning as the birds flock to water each morning.

new rule will bring, he sees a future of a South Africa that works . . . because it must. It's easier for a man to believe in miracles when his own life has been one—or does the belief manifest the miracles?

Below us, a pair of pointers sifts through the scents permeating the grass and short scrub. Their quest—and ours—is a partridge-sized bird called the greywing francolin. They're covey risers that play the angles better

than a seasoned Machiavellian. The land is too desolate to be remote. That is its charm. The birds are the alibis we need to spend time in such solitary places.

Also enjoying the view is Beau Turner and his fiancée, Gannon Hunt, a gregarious young couple who share our penchant for strong flying birds, pointing dogs, and guns that digest pellets. Beau is the youngest in a family headed by his famous father, Ted.

Find the right watering hole and you'll find unmatched sandgrouse gunning. The birds sometimes fly in flocks numbering 200 or more each morning.

Beyond the fortune, the glamour, and the hobnobbing with celebrities, Beau is the product of a complex family where answering to the chairman of the board was a daily occurrence growing up. Gannon is a gracious and lovely woman with eyes blue enough to melt the heart of a pawnbroker. Purdey's never produced a finer matched pair.

I've always been fond of bird hunting because of the people attracted to the sport.

There's no interest among this crowd in calculating the experience in pounds of meat harvested or in length of horns. As much as I enjoy occasional forays to mountain slopes for elk or to the bottomlands for deer, I simply relish the distance from telephones and the freedom of being incommunicado that is so often requisite for big-game hunting in wild country. That is what I like about Africa as well. Tell a person you're going to Canada or Europe and

he or she still expects to be able to reach you. Let the same person know that you'll be in Africa and he'll respond with, "Call me when you get back and we'll talk."

Satellite phones be damned.

From the mountain slopes of South Africa's Eastern Cape, we board a King Air

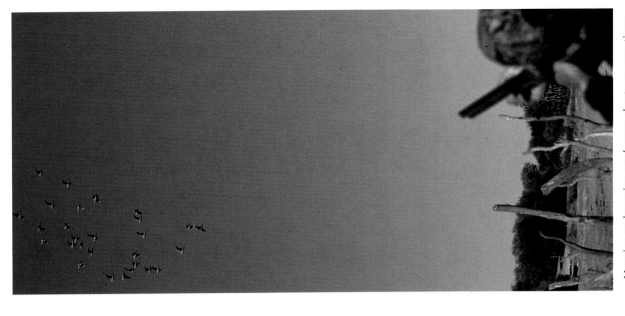

Morning and evening sandgrouse shoots are sometimes short-lived but can often produce hot-barreled gunning.

charter to the Kalahari, a name that rolls off the tongue and is synonymous with Africa. It is a vast land of sand, rock, and scrub. It's the home of the Bushmen, arguably the greatest hunters to walk the planet. I often muse how they might look upon such things as a big-game record book; Rowland Ward has no special designation for trophies taken with a spear or dart or in self-defense. The Bushmen are people whose position in the food chain changes depending on the other predators in the immediate vicinity.

We, however, have come to see about the sandgrouse. It is a word that has no singular meaning because the birds are forever found in flocks. It is unclear to me if they are even able to fly solo. When airborne, the birds often move the way a school of ocean fish twists, dives, and turns in unison. I wonder if their reflexes are that instantaneous or if they possess collective intelligence?

Sandgrouse gunning can be as sporty as any wingshooting . . . or not. The birds fly in such tight formations that a flock-shot often renders multiple grouse. Concentrate on a bird at the fringe of the flock, however, and you will have surrendered the edge to the grouse. The locals say that seven out of ten cartridges spent will be for effect only. From my experience, that might be optimistic.

There are many species of sandgrouse—

some fly to water in the morning, some in the evening—but they all must drink daily. In a desert environment, their options are limited. Knowing where the water pans are located is where professional hunter Herb Friedel, an old friend of Alistair's, comes in. He has been scouting each morning in advance of our arrival, sitting near a pool of water the size of a putting green to watch for visiting flights of grouse.

His reports suggest that our timing is good, so we position ourselves in a triangle around the water. By 9 A.M., Gannon greets the first flight by intercepting a bird with one of two shots from her 28 bore. The flight builds in a crescendo. What started as shooting every 10 or 15 minutes becomes a consistent battery.

I pause to watch the spectacle with Alistair, who recalls the days when they shot the birds year round. As damaging as that practice might have been, no one knew then the impact on the birds' populations. He shakes his head in disgust at the practice now: sandgrouse with young wade into the shallows, soaking their feathers to take water back to the chicks. Shoot a nesting bird and you have signed the death sentence for its young just as surely as killing a spawning fish breaks a genetic chain. That fact, and perhaps a twinge of guilt, has led Alistair to personally finance research on a variety of African game birds.

Alistair McLean prepares to intercept an escaping Swainson's francolin on the Springbok Flats located north of Johannesburg.

Professional dog trainer Dave Fowler enjoys the fruits of his labors as he is just a step away from unearthing a Swainson's francolin.

THE WORLD'S GREATEST WINGSHOOTING DESTINATIONS

Our drive back to camp proves a chance to spy some of the region's big game. A lone sable bull with its ebony coat, white-painted face, and sweeping antennae-like horns is the most captivating specimen among the water-buck, kudu, impala, and warthog gallery that crosses our path. It's the chance to view the abundance of big game, perhaps above all else, that distinguishes the African wingshooting experience from that of any other destination in the world.

That and the sounds of the night.

The final leg of our three-stop tour takes us to the Springbok Flats, a plain of bushveld located north of Johannesburg, Africa's only modern gateway. Waiting for us is Alistair's son Alexander and daughter Delia, who have been busy completing a new lodge to accommodate visiting wingshooters. It is just another of Alistair's dreams that he has seen come true—one that he hopes to be a chain his son will continue to lengthen. Also joining us is Dave Fowler, a family friend whose passion, and profession, is training bird dogs. Despite enduring a quadruple bypass a couple of years earlier, Dave prowls the bush with his dogs at a pace few others can match—me included. He

is living testament to the wonders of modern medicine. I hadn't seen Dave in several years, and after hearing of his health troubles, I had wondered if I ever would again. I greet him with a bear hug . . . one that means more than it once did.

We are privileged to be hunting behind Dave's dogs, a brace of pointers whose sole ambition in life is to come nose-to-nose with francolin. It's hard not to envy such singleness of purpose, such utter devotion to a simple goal. They course a field of knee-high grass that is bordered by nearly impenetrable acacias with so many thorns that they resemble castings of oversized porcupines. Birds that reach the bush are safe to fly another day.

African hunting is most romanticized for its element of danger—all manner of beasts that have been known, from time to time, to bite, claw, or stomp visitors without regard to social status. Of those tourists who perish in Africa, most die of stupidity. For the bird hunter, however, there is another, more real hazard. It comes in the form of holes dug by honey badgers. Some of these tunnels plunge vertically for 3 or 4 feet and are just large enough to swallow a man in one step. Many are well camouflaged, too, covered by a screen of grass that makes one's plummet all the more surprising. Such was the case as I

approached one of the pointers making game. One moment I was fixated on the dog, the next instant I was on my face, waist deep in a spider hole of sorts. The snapping sound in my ankle let me know that my bird hunt was over . . . at least for the day.

I hobbled back to the Land Rover and waited for the rest of the party to finish the morning shoot. Alistair, however, decided to drive me back to the lodge, where the chef also happened to be a paramedic who soon wrapped my sprain in pity and served it to me sunny-side up. All cheer aside, however, two days of watching others hunt birds proved a form of torture I mercifully had managed to avoid up till now. I felt like I was having some kind of dog nightmare where I'm a pup stuck in a crate in the back of a pickup while having to watch my littermates as they are allowed to hunt. As with such a dog, my whimpers and twitches go unheeded as well.

Fortunately, Alistair stocks a complete medical kit—gin being the handiest of the painkillers. Being a consummate host, he joins me with a glass of Scottish single malt. We toast the safari while being hypnotized by a glowing fire inside his spacious lodge. Somewhere the ghost of a Scotsman is smiling on his son, for one generation has made all the difference.

Red-billed francolin (Pternistes adspersus).

CHAPTER 10

An Okavango Oasis
~ BOTSWANA ~

Depending on how one looks at a frontier town, Maun, Botswana, has either come a long way or gone too far. For the old-guard professional hunters, the character of this outpost on the edge of the great Okavango Delta has been lost forever. Dirt roads have been paved, saloons are now cafes, and many people now hunt with cameras instead of rifles. To an American suburbanite, however, it's not a stretch of the imagination to picture the village as a part of old Africa—a time when few people made it to the Dark Continent, but many dreamed of one day walking amid the riches of her game fields.

I carried that dream with me as I met Mike Gunn at the slick of asphalt that passes for the Maun airstrip. Gunn is a 43-year-old professional hunter who—like so many whites—left Rhodesia after the bloody war that preceded that country's transformation to Zimbabwe. Gunn's rugged, 6-foot 2-inch frame, auburn beard, and sun-dried skin make him appear a native of the bush—if not a part of its wildlife.

We load my gear into a Land Rover for the three-hour dive to Chitabe One,

Swainson's francolin possess switchblade-like spurs that are nearly the size of those found on a mature tom turkey.

a camp situated in the Okavango Delta, one of the wildest regions on the planet. The Okavango River winds though Angola and then Namibia before it forms the Okavango Panhandle in northern Botswana. From there, it spills into the desert to form a great delta, its waters dying of thirst before ever meandering to a sea. It is an artery of life in an otherwise parched landscape. A complex food chain thrives within the delta, creating an Eden unlike any other this side of the Old Testament.

Elephants clearly abound in the delta as we cross their spoor perhaps an hour before actually spying one of the pachyderms. I'd seen elephants in zoos, of course, and on a couple of game ranches in South Africa, but this was different. No fence. Nothing but the largest animals to roam the world, wandering about their native habitat like prehistoric relics. This is the Africa of my imagination: wild, free, and altogether intoxicating.

Each bend in the trail brings more life. We're greeted by the vanilla and mocha of a herd of zebra; then several wildebeest with their idiotic head-nods stagger across the trail in front of us, delaying our journey. A half-

Swainson's (left) and crested francolin are just two species of game birds found in the game-rich Okavango Delta.

hour later, we spy giraffes pursing acacia leaves with their camel-like lips, careful to extract the chlorophyll without the thorns.

By late afternoon, we reach Chitabe, a canvas community on the edge of reality. The camp is covered by sausage trees with their ample fruit dangling ominously overhead. Just beyond the tents stretches a lengthy lagoon where a pair of pygmy geese swim between the pond lilies. Past them a pair of buffalo—probably outcast bulls, each with a massive boss—graze lazily like guardians at the gate of the delta's riches. The region is resplendent with life—everywhere there are animals or signs of them.

Mark Kyriachou, who owns and operates his safari business in the Okavango, greets me. He's a small-framed Greek with Einstein eyebrows who has grown up in the African bush. He's a link to Old Africa and the big-game safari tradition popularized by writer Robert Ruark during his adventures with Harry Selby. Kyriachou worked for Selby, the legendary professional hunter who many still regard as the dean of the fraternal order of big-bore toters.

There's barely time before dinner to unpack and grab a sundowner before parking

The take from a morning of beating the jungle-like "islands" of cover scattered throughout the delta. In this part of the world, one never knows what might be driven from cover.

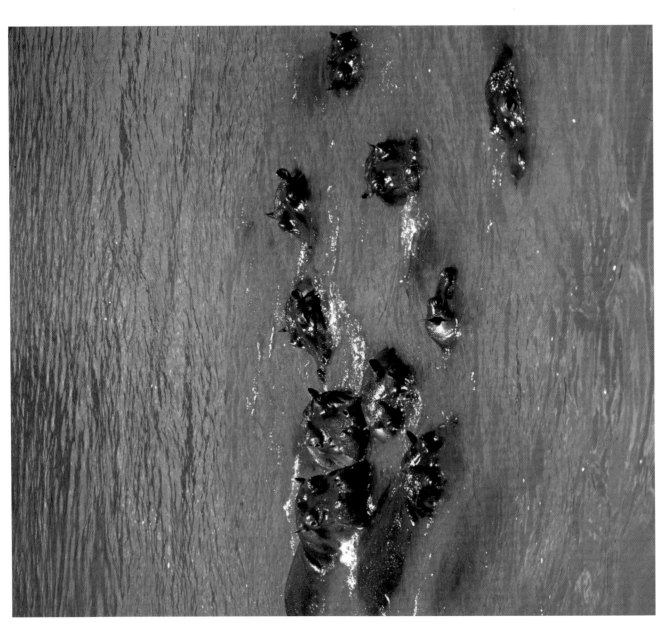

ourselves around the campfire, that most pleasant of safari habitats. I've stared into the flames of many African campfires, and conversations seem inevitably to flow from memorable hunts to great safari writers to the future of Africa and her wildlife. The same somber tone eventually permeates the discussion, an emotion evoked from the sense that the Africa that first seduced us is vanishing piecemeal like a treasure stolen with every blink. There is an almost sick urgency that one must go to Africa now, for she may be gone tomorrow. It is as if the *Mona Lisa* is about to be sold in a private auction . . . book your tickets to Paris before your chance to see her is forever lost.

As with so many African nations, Botswana's greatest immediate concern is the seemingly contradictory ravages of AIDS and overpopulation. The country's population has more than doubled since Jimmy Carter took office as president of the United States in 1977. The concept of marketing wildlife tourism tomorrow has little meaning to a man driven to feed his family today. The upshot is

Right: Seemingly sublime plant eaters, hippos are among the most dangerous of all African animals. Get between them and water and you're asking for trouble.

Opposite page: A pair of Botswana bulls test their mettle while cooling off before sunset. I photographed the encounter from a boat about 40 yards away.

Above top: Find the right water hole in the delta and you'll encounter seemingly endless flights of sandgrouse. Mixed with the sandgrouse are often swarms of doves that can quickly turn a gun barrel branding-iron-hot.

Above bottom: Sandgrouse returning to a watering hole. The birds come to drink only once a day. If they are nesting, they will wade into the water and carry the liquid on their feathers back to the awaiting chicks.

Right: The partridge-sized crested francolin are extremely vocal birds—their raucous calls can be heard throughout much of southern Africa each morning.

Crested francolin (Francolinus sephaena).

AN OKAVANGO OASIS (BOTSWANA)

101

that wildlife, and the habitat it needs to survive, is being sacrificed to feed the ever-expanding human population. This trend cannot continue indefinitely. Despite the many horrors of war and famine that have plagued Africa for generations, there is growing fear that they pale in comparison to the pestilence that awaits a continent seemingly on a collision course with a tragic fate.

Confident that Africa won't disappear while we sleep, however, we amble to the dining tent to revel in our position atop the food chain. The faint *whoo-o-o-ps* of hyenas can be heard over the din of conversation, the clinking of forks and plates, and the rumbling of stomachs beginning to ruminate. Black servants in white gowns tend to the moment's concerns—more wine and additional servings. Dessert and a final glass of port send me to that agreeable state that is halfway between consciousness and sleep.

Left: A spurwing surveys its surroundings on an Okavango flat. The birds get their name from the small horn-like protrusions found on their wings.

Opposite page: Bird shooting in Africa is about so much more than pulling the trigger: nowhere else in the world can one be gunning doves in the morning and walking among the elephants in the afternoon.

Old friend Joe Coogan watches for doves in the shadow of a baobab, a tree that looks as if it's been turned upside down to expose its roots skyward.

The Rover splashes axle-deep in a finger of the delta's water that looks almost streamlike as we leave camp for a drive-about in search of francolin. There are three predominant varieties of the ground-dwelling birds in the region: red-billed, crested, and Swainson's. Francolin exist over much of sub-Saharan Africa and come in dozens of species, ranging from the quail-sized coqui to the Cape francolin, which is nearly the size of a pheasant.

Dogs are difficult to keep in the region because leopards regularly patrol camp at night and have difficulty distinguishing pets from easy prey. The flat plain of the delta is punctuated by the occasional copse of palm and thick scrub, the kind of habitat that provides the francolin an ideal escape from the intensity of the midday sun and a roosting place for fish eagles that fly sorties over the area. It is in these islands of cover that our bird hunting takes place.

Gunn instructs the staff of five beaters to encircle one of the patches of bush and drive it toward the two of us waiting at the opposite end—I hold a 12-gauge over-and-under with Italian loads of 7 1/2 shot. Gunn grips a bolt-action .458 with 500-grain bullets— insurance against any surprise flushes. Shouts and claps grow ever louder as the line of beaters draw midway through the cover. Their approach is marked by the scurrying

A red-billed francolin perches on a termite mound in the Okavango Delta. Redbills provide the lion's share of upland bird gunning in the region. Given the extensive number of predators in the area (e.g., leopards, lions, hyenas) it's very difficult to keep bird dogs in the delta.

forms of francolin that resemble Japanese running from Godzilla in one of those "B" movies where the actors' lip movements never match the words being spoken.

The first bird to take flight sails 30 yards to my right, climbing steadily until it absorbs the punch of my shot. Three more birds follow the same course. Two fold. A half-dozen more launch as my gun is broken and I'm fumbling for shells as though searching for exact change. I intercept the last of the six-bird covey. Another pair flush to the left, quartering out the back door. I ignore a mother warthog and her four piglets that bolt—tails erect—10 feet to my right and pluck the closest bird from the air. The beaters take pride in the successful ambush, knowing that a surplus of game meat will mean protein in their otherwise starchy diets.

We reload the Rover, with guns and bodies protruding like a banana republic hit squad. We repeat the strategy, though we choose to tackle a larger stand of jungle this time. Gunn and I again take our position at the end of the cover, waiting to reap the harvest delivered by the beaters. Soon after the drive begins, however, the shouting of the staff turns to screams. Gunn steps forward,

pulling his .458 off his shoulder at the same moment. In nearly the same instant, a cow and a calf elephant emerge from the bush, the matriarch's trunk in the air as she quarters toward our end.

"Come quickly," shouts Gunn as we dash at a right angle from the beasts. Storming elephants move as unpredictably as plains twisters do, so Gunn is eager to give the pachyderms a wide berth. I'm suddenly feeling decidedly undergunned, armed with only the bird loads, but I retain my sense of humor as I can't help but think of Sean Connery's unforgettable line in *The Untouchables*, "Leave it to a dago to bring a knife to a gunfight."

The elephants thunder past, melting surprisingly quickly into the surrounding bush. What amazes the first-time visitor to elephant country is just how well such an enormous beast can cloak itself in the shadows. The francolin hunt suddenly becomes anticlimactic, upstaged by the drama and adrenaline induced by the tuskers.

A plume of smoke billows on the horizon as Gunn peers through his binoculars. There is

a strangeness about this smoke; it lingers long and ghostlike in the air. Gunn and I climb aboard the Rover to investigate. A quarter-mile away and it becomes clear that this isn't smoke at all, but rather a cloud of dust blown to the sky by a herd of some 2,000 stampeding buffalo. It's a mass of game unlike any I've ever seen—even surpassing the great caribou migrations that I've witnessed in the Canadian Arctic.

Trailing the herd is a pride of seven lions, working the buffalo like a shepherd might his flock. Three enormous bulls stay to the rear of the herd, turning to face the oncoming lions without fear. "They look at you as though you owe them money," wrote Ruark in *Hour of the Hunter* of the Cape buffalo's contemptuous stare. In *African Twilight* novelist Robert F. Jones simply described them as "mean as a half-ton hemorrhoid," characterizations any lion no doubt would confirm.

We watch in wonder for more than an hour as the lions' advances are thwarted by the buffalo that seem to view the cats as little more than irritations in their otherwise sublimely bovine existence. It is the picture of the Africa I've forever dreamed, one that will remain in my memory . . . perhaps long after

it has disappeared from the landscape.

Part Three

An Addiction of Birds

For the adventuresome wingshooter, South America/Mexico exists as a seductress of sorts. Her endless flocks of doves and ducks tempt shotgunners from across the globe with the promise of unimaginable gunning. The danger of one trip to the bird fields of Argentina, Uruguay, or Colombia is that one's appreciation of the local dove shoot or opening day of duck season could forever be tainted. It is as if there is a fear that one could develop a dependency on such shooting—as if there is no going back after a taste of the forbidden fruit. Wingshooting writers often emphasize that it's not the number of shots taken that matters, but how one views the quality of the experience. To a degree, such a mantra is unarguable. However, there are shoots . . . and then there are, *Holy Christ, have you ever seen so many birds!* shoots.

What is certain is that trying to equate U.S. hunting seasons and bag limits with the Latin American experience is a foolhardy and myopic endeavor. When on the pampas, do as the dove gunners do.

Much of South America is a mosaic of land with the perfect balance of food, cover, and water needed for growing unfathomable numbers of doves, pigeons, ducks, and geese. No matter how puritanical a soul, it is difficult not to let the Latin American wingshooting experience consume you like an addiction of sorts.

Most notable on any Latin American wingshooting tour is Argentina, a country where bird hunters pause from shooting only long enough to feast on grilled beef in portions that could satiate a rugby team's appetite and a vascular surgeon's bank account. Indeed, *vino tinto* consumption has a medicinal purpose. From Magellan and ashy-headed geese in the south to rosy-billed ducks and silver teal in the north, Argentina offers the most spectacular waterfowling in the world. The vast expanse of wetlands found across northern Argentina and southern Brazil's Pantanal regions consists of a duck nursery rivaled only by the famous prairie pothole country of the Dakotas and western Canada.

In the 1960s and '70s, demand in Europe for Patagonian fox furs grew voraciously. Consequently, all manner of trappers and hunters pursued the animals in an effort to meet the demand. The result was that the chief predator of the Magellan geese had been diminished from the landscape, opening the door to a goose population explosion of historic proportions. Overwhelmed by the geese, grain farmers struggled to cope with the hungry birds as they consumed their livelihoods like feathered locusts. Desperate to control the birds, farmers even resorted to poison, killing tens of thousands of the geese and bulldozing the carcasses into ditches. Rice farmers to the north experienced similar problems with ducks that found the abundant supply of rice irresistible. The rice growers, too, poisoned flocks en masse. Moreover, swarms of doves and pigeons reached plague-like levels, devouring entire crops overnight. Thus, the stage was set for developing a wingshooting infrastructure across the country to turn problem birds into an economic resource to attract badly needed foreign currency.

For upland hunting aficionados, the perdiz, or tinamou, gunning over well-trained pointing dogs makes a stroll over open pasturelands a welcome diversion from the stationary duck, goose, and dove shooting. These partridge-sized birds hold well for points and rocket from sparse cover, providing shooting as electrifying as any found the world over.

Although Argentina is the brightest star in the brilliant constellation that is Latin American wingshooting, Uruguay's dove and pigeon shooting rivals the best of the gunning found throughout Argentina. Moreover, Colombia's legendary Cauca

Valley remained the world's hottest dove-shooting destination throughout the 1970s and early '80s, and is still a viable—albeit diminished—location for the birds. Exploratory trips made to Ecuador and Peru in the late 1990s might one day yield commercial-quality wingshooting as well

for both doves and perdiz.

Closer than Africa, less expensive than Europe, and without the jet-lag-inducing time changes of destinations overseas, Latin America has risen to the top of the international wingshooting scene—a spot it is likely to retain for many years to come.

AN ADDICTION OF BIRDS

109

Black brant (Branta bernicla nigricans).

A Postcard from South of the Border

⌘ MEXICO ⌘

hat seems an endless stream of pintails wafts like feathered smoke high over my blind, the trill of their whistles barely audible over the drone of so many wingbeats. The small ring of mangrove stems stuck in the mud around me serves as both my blind and a door into North America's greatest duck concentrations. The funnel of the continent's major wildfowl flyways leads to the rich coastal estuaries of America's southern neighbor, and waterfowlers who venture to the fabled land of the Yaqui Indians will taste the intoxicating flavor of the region's legendary wingshooting.

In addition to the phenomenal numbers of ducks found here, there is an impressive array of species: pintails; Pacific brant; gadwall; wigeon; blue-winged, green-winged, and cinnamon teal; fulvous and black-bellied tree ducks; redheads; greater scaup; shovelers; mottled or Mexican ducks; canvasbacks; and many others. The same estuaries that serve as winter havens for ducks also host pelicans, herons, oyster-catchers, spoonbills, terns, gulls, and myriad diminutive shorebirds that all travel here to feed on the rich salsa of fish, aquatic invertebrates, and insects that thrive in the brackish waters.

Partners Ruben del Castillo and Miguel Puig are two English-speaking

Given the shallow flats surrounding Tobari Bay, an airboat is the best mode of transport to and from the mangrove blinds used in this part of Mexico.

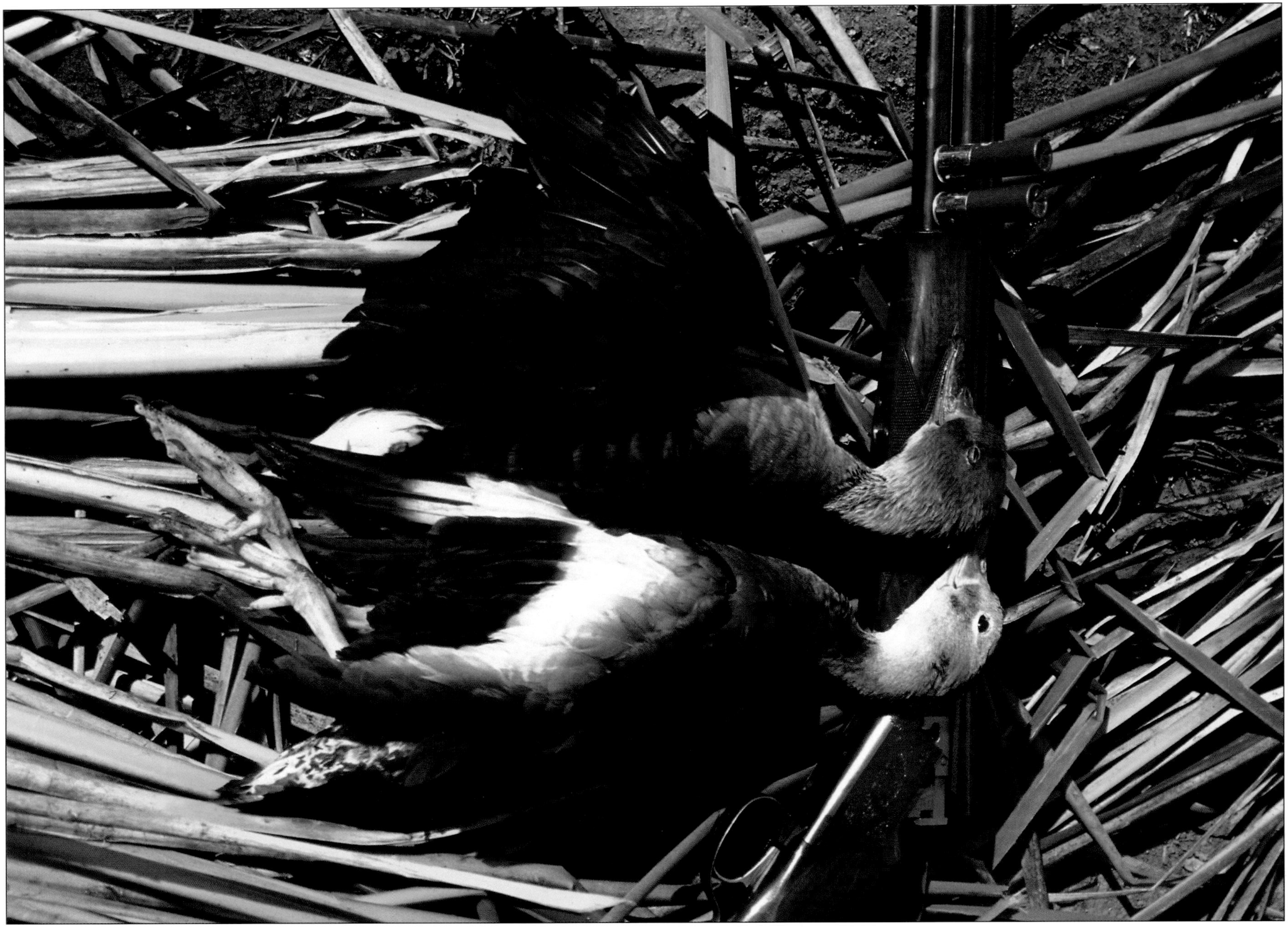

Mexicans who have made it their business to help gringos sample the best of Mexico's wing-shooting. Their Wingshooters Lodge (formerly Mex-Bass Outfitters) has become a favorite destination for dove and duck hunters. Because of its close proximity and generous bird supply, Mexico annually hosts as many as 4,000 U.S. duck hunters—making it among the most popular foreign destination for U.S. shooters. Unforgettable waterfowling opportunities exist in several Mexican states, though Sinaloa is probably the nation's best duck-hunting state. For wingshooters who are looking for the varied gunning offered in a combination duck-and-dove adventure, however, the mixed-bag opportunities found in Sonora's Yaqui Valley simply are astounding.

My first taste of this celebrated wingshooting came while sharing a blind with Ruben del Castillo on an afternoon hunt on Tobari Bay—an inlet off the Gulf of California. Though excellent waterfowl numbers are still found in the vicinity, there were considerably more

Left: After spending a morning duck hunting along the coast, gunners visiting Wingshooters Lodge have the chance to head to harvested grain fields, where they can enjoy hot-barreled gunning for the region's aerobatic doves.

Opposite page: The freshwater lagoons near the Mexican community of Ciudad Obregón hold thousands of black-bellied and fulvous whistling ducks. With long necks and legs, the ducks appear like shorebirds in flight.

their determination to reach the spread evident by the directness of their course to us. The gusts force them to fly at cropduster altitude, buzzing the mangrove tops as they swing briefly over land to reach us. We take a pair of drakes from the flock, expending an equal number of shots. Duck hunting in Mexico affords the shooter the opportunity to be selective. With nearly continual flights streaming past our blind, there is no urgency that the birds might disappear any time soon. We are careful to pick drakes from the flocks and seldom shoot more than once or twice at any given flight. With a generous limit and an ample supply of birds, selective shooting is a grand way to extend the hunting experience.

A long line of Pacific black brant soon decoy behind the wigeon, tapping the air currents ever so slightly with their wing tips as they coast like feathered kites to the decoys. I intercept a pair while Ruben does the same. The birds are moving into the bay as the outgoing tide exposes the area's mudflats, enticing resting and feeding locations for the brant. Pacific brant are tidewater geese that nest in the high arctic along the coasts of Canada and Alaska. A small percentage of the 150,000 brant found in the Pacific Flyway also nest on Vrangelya Island in what was formerly the Soviet Union. Baja California and the northwest coast of Mexico—some 3,000 miles from

Fulvous whistling duck (Dendrocygna bicolor).

birds in the Yaqui Valley in the 1950s, when rice was the major crop of the region. Since that time, the Alvaro Obregón Dam has been built, and its construction—along with an extensive series of new irrigation canals—diverted water across nearly the entire valley. Since the limited water supply is now spread throughout a vast region, there no longer are ample reserves to sustain the flooding needed for the rice farms that once used much of the available water in the valley. Instead, crops such as wheat and safflower now dominate the area that has come to be known as Mexico's breadbasket.

Today, the ducks loaf by day in the estuaries lining the Gulf of California, a pool of water formerly known as the Sea of Cortez. This body of water begins below Mexicali and stretches some 700 miles south to Mazatlan. At twilight, the ducks leave the waters en masse to feed on the surrounding grain fields, much to the chagrin of area farmers. Such food supplies in close proximity to resting waters allow the birds to fatten themselves before their return journeys north to the breeding grounds.

Tide-hopping is the rule to waterfowling here. It's common to start the day with a dove shoot and end it with a duck hunt. A break for steak fajitas, grilled duck, chicken enchiladas, and other memorable entrées is sandwiched between the hunts with plenty of time for that most celebrated of Mexican pastimes, the siesta.

Surrounding our blind are some 20 pintail decoys, listing slightly in the waves borne of the winds off the gulf. A flock of perhaps 40 wigeon fight the breeze toward our decoys,

A flock of fulvous whistling ducks heads for a freshwater marsh. The unique call of these ducks is unmistakable . . . and unforgettable. (Photo by Gary Kramer.)

brant nesting grounds—represent the two premier regions in which to hunt Pacific brant.

Ruben and I greet flights of brant with intermittent shots as I continue my introduction to this intriguing bird. These diminutive sea geese, with their dusky plumage, are uniquely linked to the ebb and flow of the ocean—feeding at low tide on the beds of exposed eelgrass. During the incoming tide, the birds congregate in large rafts in the midst of bays, often out of reach of hunters. Low tide, then, is the period when waterfowlers enjoy their best chances of encountering brant within shotgun range. One brant that folds to my shot was banded some four years earlier, 22 miles southeast of Lonely, Alaska. Another brant, taken by a different member of the group, proves nearly 20 years old, according to banding data. Such a bird probably logged as many as 120,000 miles in its lifetime of migrations.

In addition to the brant, we take a few wigeon and pintails that make up the preponderance of the other species winging past our blind. We watch flock upon flock of wigeon sail over our blocks and land nearby, until some 2,000 birds float outside the perimeter of our decoys like a moat made of pinions. We look to diversify our take and decide to wait for a redhead, a canvasback, or perhaps a cinnamon teal to cross our path. The hiatus in the activity isn't long as a lone drake cin-

Black brant make an arduous migratory journey from their breeding waters along the coast of Alaska to the warm waters of coastal Mexico. In the process of making the 3,000-mile foray, they'll lose some 40 percent of their body weight.

namon teal splashes among the flock of wigeon outside our decoy spread, its russet plumage looking like a sparkling ruby against a bed of dull gravel.

I watch intently for 20 minutes as the ducks swim about, oblivious to our blind. Finally, in an act of fate unprecedented in my waterfowling career, the flock rises in unison flying over our blind, giving me the opportunity to surgically pluck the lone cinnamon teal

A banded brant is a rare trophy. This brant turned out to be at least 10 years old, having logged more than 60,000 miles while making its annual migratory treks.

found in the marshes near Obregón, a prosperous city of 400,000 inhabitants that lies some 20 miles inland from Tobari Bay. Though hunters will encounter a few of these birds near the coastal estuaries, the tree ducks are more regularly seen on the freshwater marshes farther inland.

We drive some 25 miles east of Obregón on the last morning of my wingshooting foray to Mexico. At the end of our drive is a series of small cattail sloughs, preferred habitat for the tree ducks. As we approach the first marsh, at least 500 *pichiguilas*—both fulvous and black-bellied—spook from the water and begin circling the marsh, creating a chorus of their characteristic whistling noises that proves reminiscent of an unruly crowd at a tennis match. In flight, the long legs of these ducks dangle awkwardly behind them, giving the birds a strange, almost shorebird appearance. Their unique flying form—a silhouette elongated by the bird's stretched neck and trailing legs—can make them deceptive targets as well.

The dramatic sights and sounds of thousands of the birds lifting off that small marsh rimmed by house-high cattails will live in my mind's eye, next to parts of my soul that store the feeling of sheer awe and inspiration that occur when one witnesses such concentrations of wildfowl.

Along with the other waterfowl common to this expanse of Mexico, I've forever had a fascination for stalking the unique tree ducks, or *pichiguilas*, that inhabit the region. Both the fulvous and black-bellied tree duck can be

from the massive congregation of wigeon. I quickly retrieve the bird and examine its contrasting red and blue plumage with the admiration of someone who seldom sees this beautiful duck of the West.

Waterfowlers visiting the coastal marshes of Tobari Bay will marvel at the amount of bird life found in this rich environment. Many of the Pacific Flyway's ducks and shorebirds find their way to these fragile tidal estuaries.

THE WORLD'S GREATEST WINGSHOOTING DESTINATIONS

118

CHAPTER 12

A Shower of Pintails
～ MEXICO ～

o matter which way I turn, there are flocks of pintails dressed in their full nuptial tuxedos. They crisscross the sky in lines, their wings flapping through thermals like the waving legs of feathered centipedes. We're hoping for new birds on the heels of an arctic blast that dumped enough snow to cover even the tallest cowboy boots as far south as the Texas Panhandle just a few days earlier. The sprigs passing overhead are no doubt en route to one of the countless shallow bays that make up the 4,000-square-mile Lake Guerrero. Many of these beds are choked with smartweed, one of the most addictive substances known to ducks. In the deeper water hydrilla is plentiful, and the crustaceans that cling to it are preferred by the thousands of scaup, canvasbacks, and ringnecks that spend the winter on this inland sea located just 130 miles south of the Texas line.

In addition to the puzzle of pintails above my blind, occasional flights of greenwing, bluewing, and cinnamon teal bank past me—mostly going unnoticed until any chance of intercepting them is gone in a blink. Teal don't so much decoy as they appear. Tilt your head down just long enough to pour a cup of coffee or

There's no bird so elegant as the pintail in flight. It's sleek design makes it a marvel in the air, and there's no better place to find them than the waters of Lake Guerrero. (Photo by Bill Buckley.)

dry the reeds in your duck calls and teal will often materialize and vanish like birds in some sort of virtual reality game. Their modus operandi of hopscotching over cattail stands or clumps of rushes as they fly the perimeter of a marsh frequently keeps them hidden until one is lucky to fire even a quick shot in desperation . . . or frustration.

Such was the case for my blind mates, Jay Logsdon and Bill Buckley, and me. Logsdon is a long-time wingshooting outfitter who has hunted extensively in Mexico. Buckley is a talented photographer whose waterfowling images have a way of distilling the essence of the sport as only a photographer who knows the game could capture. Together, we're here to investigate the opportunities that await U.S. waterfowlers and upland bird hunters—it's a calling in which we are dutifully willing to immerse ourselves.

Despite the abundance of pintails in the vicinity, the birds avoid our blind as though there is a glass dome some 80 yards above us.

Right: Blue-winged teal by the cloud can be found in the shallow expanses of Lake Guerrero. Both cinnamon and green-winged teal, however, can also be found on the lake. (Photo by Bill Buckley.)

Opposite page: In the early morning light, the dead tree branches protruding from Lake Guerrero are enough to hide a hunter's outline. (Photo by Bill Buckley.)

The Sports Afield on Assignment television crew traveled to Lake Guerrero to chronicle the area's amazing waterfowling. (Photo by Bill Buckley.)

No manner of call or shift in the decoys has any impact on these birds that have survived duck hunters from the Canadian prairies to the coastal marshes of Louisiana. No folks are better at separating ducks from sky than the Cajuns, people who frequently learn to speak mallard before they do French or English.

Resigned that we will have to sort out a radical new approach for the pintails, we instead scan the tops of the dead trees that litter the lake like the aftermath of what was a war zone, looking for passing flights of teal. Buckley plucks a cinnamon teal from a passing flock, the bird looks like a feathered ruby passing through the air—it proved to be one of several of the birds he would take in his five days of shooting both gun and camera.

Logsdon and I trip three more bluewings out of a flock that passes in front while Buckley gropes for more cartridges. It is a scenario that lasts for two hours—consistent flights of ducks, which is the hallmark of Mexican duck hunting . . . and it's what keeps luring thousands of U.S. waterfowlers across the border each year.

Logsdon and I climb aboard a small fiberglass boat piloted by Lalo, who will take us to our morning blind. The cold front that passed through yesterday has subsided, and there is little wind. The lack of gusts is a mixed blessing of sorts: nothing improves duck hunting more than blustery weather, but the same breeze can turn a boat ride on the shallow lake into a teeth-rattling adventure aboard a liquid roller coaster. I am content to let St. Hubertus serve up whatever the weather and the birds deliver. This is, after all, Mexico, where even poor duck hunts produce more birds than many good days in a U.S. duck blind.

I couldn't imagine, however, the good fortune that was about to be bestowed upon us.

Before first light, the faint forms of pintails meteoring through the sky portended events to come. No sooner had Lalo and Logsdon finished positioning the decoys than a flock of 20 pintails plummeted from the heavens in a wing-searing corkscrew descent to our spread.

It is the sort of sight that reduces even ardent waterfowlers to something akin to tail-wagging Lab pups. The birds make one last rotation around our blocks before deciding to purchase a piece of calm water inside our spread.

Logsdon has other ideas, rising up an instant before calling the shot—it's an old trick every duck hunter learns early on if he wants to ensure himself a clean shot at birds that aren't yet flaring from the shots of other gunners.

Another secret seasoned waterfowlers learn is to watch out of the corners of their eyes for movement from the person calling the shot.

The key is to rise up to fire at the same instant the blind boss begins the shooting sequence. It made little difference in this instance, however: so complete was our deception that even a five-thumbed gunner would have had time to unleash several rounds before the birds could make good their escapes.

Four stunningly beautiful sprigs fall in the volley. For a duck hunter such as me who cut his teeth on Great Lakes waterfowling, the sight of pintails the way artists paint them is like the first moment after opening a gift you've longed to receive. They are a study in perfect elegance—both in flight and in hand—right up to their chocolate heads with racing stripes and bills that look as if they've been airbrushed a gray-blue that somehow seems too brilliant to fit into nature.

There is a palpable electricity in the blind now as we are buoyed by our close-encounter with the sprigs the same way marlin fishermen toast the first billfish brought to the boat. But the ducks continued to come, another half-dozen pintail flocks surrendering some of their own to our cause. Mixed in between was a flock of some 30 black-bellied whistling ducks, green-winged teal, wigeon, and a perfect specimen mottled duck—a solitary bird that is only found along the Gulf Coast and that is nearly indistinguishable from its northern cousin, the black duck. It is the sort of rare day when all

Pintails in Mexico are fully plumed and strikingly beautiful birds. It's enough to transform any ardent waterfowler into a tail-wagging pup. (Photo by Bill Buckley.)

the forces in the duck world are conspiring to deliver birds to your blocks. It is the memory of such an experience that will forever propel a waterfowler to return to the marsh even after a prolonged dry period. Waterfowlers are nothing if not eternal optimists.

For the father-and-son tandem of Barry and Dean Putegnat, life amid the quail fields of their northern Mexico ranch is a manifestation of heaven on Earth. Their Rancho Caracol Lodge sits in foothills a short drive from abundant quail, dove, duck, and goose hunting. A few minutes below the lodge is a private lake teaming with largemouth bass and even a handful of landlocked tarpon that have existed in the lake since its creation 30 years ago.

In an afternoon spent walking the fields and hedgerows of a nearby farm on which the Putegnats hunt, we encountered a dozen coveys—most of which launched from in front of one of the Putegnats' skilled pointing dogs. There is no more genteel form of hunting than bobwhites over staunch pointers.

"I was once told that when a hunter has tried most forms of hunting," says Barry, "he will eventually return to pointing dogs and quail."

As the afternoon light painted the grass, mesquite, and cactus in a golden hue, Sam, a liver-and-white pointer, loped along in a nonchalant manner. In an instant, however, the dog skidded sideways as it caught a tendril of scent wafting from a covey pinned under a small pile of branches at the base of a nearby tree. I eased in front of the dog as it peered back and forth from me to the scent of the birds as if he were nodding to me that I ought to hurry up and flush the birds already. I obliged. Perhaps 15 birds burst out of the cover, swinging over a cut sorghum field. My first barrel took a bird quickly while the second dropped a pair of birds in one shot as they happened to cross paths about 35 yards out. It is the only Scotch double on wild birds ever in my upland gunning career, and it seemed only a fitting piece of perfection to a trip to paradise.

Rosy-billed pochard (Netta peposaca).

CHAPTER 13

The World's Finest Fowling
~ ARGENTINA ~

aterfowlers subsist on a diet of memories and anticipation. That axiom comes to mind as I stand knee-deep in water and enthusiasm. I spin back and forth, capturing glimpses of ducks in small flocks as they swim the air currents over the decoys in front of me. The constant trill of pintails whistles across the marsh, sounding like a cricket perched atop my shoulder. A strange cacophony of sounds precedes the rapture of dawn as if an orchestra consisting of unknown instruments is tuning up for a performance.

With stars in the eastern sky washed by the first light of the morning, perhaps 2,000 ducks lift off and begin flying the perimeter of the 100-acre rush-collared wetland. Hundreds of birds discover the decoys and plummet, stopping short of committing to set their wings. In moments, it becomes impossible to track all the inbound birds—like an air-traffic controller's nightmare. My first shots are laughably behind their targets, but the gunfire sends a stunning aggregation of ducks and other birds into the air, the sight resembling the mushroom plume of a nuclear detonation on the horizon. Instantly, the skies are littered with twittering wings.

The Duncans in a moment of repose following a morning duck shoot near Colonel Suarez. The estancia has a classic South American hunting motif to welcome visiting hunters.

127

Above: Argentina's many quality vintages are a perfect way to toast the end of a successful hunt. Here, visiting Mississippi hunter Tom Duncan surrenders to the hospitality of our Argentinean hosts.

Right: Rosy-billed pochards are the most sought after ducks in Argentina. They are mallard-sized birds that readily decoy.

Above: Scores of Spanish-style estancias (ranches) are found throughout Argentina. This is Sam Jose, a handsome retreat located near some of the best Magellan goose-hunting I've ever experienced in Argentina.

Left: A pair of cinnamon teal buzz the decoys as guide Alexander Antonin tries to catch up to them. These are the same cinnamon teal that breed and nest near the Great Salt Lake in Utah. The birds make an extraordinarily long migration all the way to central South America.

A flock of rosy-billed pochards, looking like greater scaup, passes 25 yards over the decoys. I lead the first bird, and at the slap of my trigger, the third bird in line falls.

"Nice shot," hollers guide Alexander Antonin. I nod and smile in appreciation. There will be enough misses ahead . . . no need to make myself look any worse than necessary, I reason.

A flock of 20 or so white-faced whistling ducks hiss their consternation at having to vacate their once quiet confines. They head for

Above: The farm fields around the town of Colonel Suarez in western Argentina support huge numbers of Magellan geese, providing spectacular gunning for visiting wingshooters.

Right: White-faced whistling ducks (upper left), Chiloe wigeon, and rosy-billed pochards were just some of the many species taken while hunting in central Argentina.

Opposite page: Windsocks and silhouette decoys planted amid this picked cornfield proved all the incentive necessary to attract flock upon flock of abundant Magellan geese.

The Duncans wait until the last possible moment to surprise these incoming Magellan geese. The birds see little hunting pressure, so they decoy with gusto.

any of countless small marshes and ponds in the sprawling, flat plains of western Argentina. Save for the occasional copse of eucalyptus and wandering gaucho, the region's open terrain could be easily confused for much of the Dakotas.

Before the whistlers dissolve off my radar screen, a dozen Chiloe wigeon decide to inspect my decoys more closely, setting their wings like their North American counterparts duped by a seductive spread of mallard blocks. I splash a brace, doing the wader waltz through the water to recover the downed birds so that I might examine the ducks more closely. Their size and conformation are similar to those of the American wigeon, but their plumage is predominantly white with an iridescent purple mask that stands in dramatic contrast to the rest of the ivory-colored feathers.

A handful of other species—most of which I've only seen on the color plates of bird books—make up our invited guests. In my mind's eye, I assign North American duck species to the silhouettes I'm seeing, an attempt to help me remember the identities of the Argentinean ducks, like some sort of picture association game. Despite the differences in birds and the miles from my home waters, a dawn punctuated by ducks forever provides the salt to flavor a waterfowler's mood.

Argentina is to waterfowling what South Dakota is to pheasant hunting, what the Madison and Bighorn are to fly-fishing, and what the Rocky Mountains are to elk hunting. It's the fowlers' El Dorado and Shangri-la rolled into one. Unfathomable numbers of birds, quality outfitters, generous limits, historic *estancias*, and accessible transportation combine to make Argentina the land upon which a growing number of wingshooters are fixing their gaze.

Our party consists of the Duncan family from Mississippi, Jim and Joyce and their son Tom. They're repeat visitors, having parlayed their success in the timber business to family outings in the land of the pampas and the gaucho. Stuart Williams, a writer who crosses oceans as frequently as others cross the street, is making his 31st trip to this hallowed wing-shooting destination with us. Boris Popov and his wife, Techana, have exchanged the cool spring of Minnesota for the comparatively warm winter of Argentina.

We divide our hunts into morning and evening affairs, leaving by 6 A.M. to reach our gunning sloughs by 6:30. Some venues come replete with sunken blinds, while others are meant for waders. The hunting is equally memorable in either case. I use a mixture of both lead and bismuth shells and am unable to discern a difference in effectiveness between the two. Flock upon flock of ducks—eight or nine different species in all—engage the decoy spread ahead of me.

INDEPENDENCE DAY

July 4 isn't thought of as a red-letter day on the waterfowler's calendar. For four gringos, however, it is a date that will forever remain indelibly etched in our waterfowling memories.

It starts with a 45-minute drive from Sam Jose, an *estancia* located near the town of Colonel Suarez in western Argentina. With only the light from the Southern Cross illuminating the sky, a team of five bird boys dig pits for the gunners and position a couple hundred windsocks and silhouette decoys like a moat of party balloons around the blinds. Hints of amber skies on the eastern horizon bring our initial visitors: a skein of 30 Magellan geese. The males are larger than snow geese but, like their North American counterparts, are also predominantly white. The females, conversely, wear a beautiful combination of chocolate-, black-, and white-barred plumage.

Taxonomically, there are no true geese in the Southern Hemisphere (except introduced Canadas in New Zealand and Australia). The Magellan geese are actually sheldgeese—one of eight species found in South America and Africa. We introduce a handful of them to the bismuth loads of number 2 shot, finding them to be as effective on these larger birds as they are on ducks.

Another dozen flocks visit us, lined up one after another like jetliners approaching O'Hare on Christmas Eve. The smell of powder turned to smoke permeates the air as the click and snap of double guns breaking and closing becomes Morse code, signaling a shoot for the ages. The concentration of birds is reminiscent of the North American plains each spring and autumn. It is the kind of abundance that staggers the imagination and decoys hunters back to Argentina.

White-faced whistling duck (Dendrocygna viduata).

CHAPTER 14

Wings Over the Pampas
ARGENTINA

ith the cityscape of Buenos Aires etched in neon in our rearview mirror, my two drivers and I begin the three-hour journey to Patria Chica, a half-century-old *estancia* located in the sprawling plains of Argentina. I crane my neck against the window of the Suburban to pay homage to the Southern Cross, a constellation upon which I first set eyes a decade earlier while floating Ecuador's Rio Napo, which feeds the Amazon and helps it become one of the world's great waterways.

The welcoming dwelling, with its whitewashed walls and hardwood trim, is situated along a great drainage system created by the Parana and Uruguay Rivers as they meander their way inexorably to the Atlantic Ocean. This massive expanse of marsh and lowland stretches for some 150 miles before emptying into the Rio de la Plata, a short-lived river that quickly surrenders its silt-laden waters to the Atlantic.

When we arrive at the *estancia* after midnight, no light could be seen for miles, save for a few stars that shown through the patchwork of clouds overhead. We've traveled beyond the reach of rural electrification, which, in the

Guide Pablo Pereira collects a brace of ducks during a morning shoot in northern Argentina.

Authentic gaucho—no Hollywood costume here. These "cowboys of the pampas" tend to flocks of sheep and cattle throughout the rich agricultural region.

estancia, begins humming and soon incandescence temporarily blinds us until we rub the sleep from our eyes. After greeting the other five U.S. shooters through the haze brought about by 12 hours of traveling followed by an early morning, we eat breakfast—or lunch or dinner depending on the time zone from which one originates—before departing in the darkness for our hunting areas near Rio Gualeguay, a river whose confluence with the Rio de la Plata forms one of the region's many alluring waterfowling locales. I had traversed some 200 miles of Argentina's outback and had yet to see anything other than the shoulders of roads illuminated by headlights whose rays were quickly swallowed by the abyss of the Argentinean night.

Such delay only heightens my anticipation of dawn—I await sunrise like the unveiling of a great work of art. Above in the darkness, the ghostly forms of ducks fly past, the peculiar three-note *tsri-tsri-tsreeo* whistles of tree ducks and the *wheeoo* chatter of rosy-billed pochards confirm that the silhouettes aren't mere illusions and that this is a long way from my home waterfowling turf, where mallards and wood ducks are the featured attractions. I am joined by Richard Mellish, one of the first Americans to explore the world of Argentina's remarkable waterfowling. He's a veteran of six Argentinean wingshooting forays and proves a valuable source of informa-

tion for my first junket to the pampas.

A distant storm sizzles with lightning streaks, too removed for their thunder to be heard from our blind. The combination of early morning sun against the bruised clouds is starkly captivating and provides a photogenic backdrop to the seemingly endless flights of

Veteran international wingshooter Richard Mellish readies for more birds as we share a blind near the Rio Gualeguay in northern Argentina.

developing world, is seldom far from the major metropolitan centers.

Sleep is foremost on my agenda as morning—such as it is for waterfowlers the world over—comes at 4:30 in the form of a firm rap on the door of my room. A propane generator, the only source of electrical power to the

ducks that course overhead. Ducks don't so much flock over the pampas as they cloud, confirming the rumors I had heard of vast riches of wildfowl below the equator.

The variety of species found in this region is as impressive as the sheer numbers of the birds. The staple of the gunning is provided by the rosy-billed pochard, a coal-black, stoutly built duck whose most distinctive feature—as its name suggests—is a red bill with a fleshy hump at its base. Like most ducks and geese found in southern South America, the rosybill migrates north during winter, finding an abundance of suitable habitat on the northern marshes. Although a handsome bird, to those who have tasted its succulent meat it is perhaps at its most beautiful when grilled medium rare and served over toast. A happy marriage occurs in the palate when the flavor of grilled pochard is mixed with any of several fine Argentinean or Chilean red wines.

Three species of tree ducks are also common here: the stunningly ornate white-faced, the fulvous, and the black-bellied. All three species commonly congregate, but the white-faced tree duck is unique in that it is found from sub-Saharan Africa to Costa Rica and

While there are large numbers of ducks throughout much of northern Argentina, it's not uncommon to experience shooting at singles and pairs—instead of large flocks.

ing shots at passing flocks of fulvous and black-bellied tree ducks.

Seemingly every acre of land is grazed in Argentina, with cattle standing knee-deep in the browsed cover of the marshes. Despite such degradation, the vastness of the wetlands has, to this point, been able to withstand the relatively primitive agricultural practices employed over much of the northern lowlands. Grain and livestock—especially beef—are the country's major exports. To the east, Uruguay is another country whose economy is largely dependent on commodity prices—including rice. Rice growers in that nation periodically poison ducks to reduce the amount of grain lost to the birds. In parts of Argentina, as well, waterfowl are poisoned in an attempt to minimize crop losses. Ducks Unlimited, through joint international efforts, has worked to convince Argentinean officials to halt the practice, citing the potential the birds have to increase the country's sporting tourism.

The great expanse of wetlands in the Gran Chaco region of northern Argentina—an area northwest of Entre Rios, the province in which we are hunting—also helps sustain the country's astounding duck populations. The region is marked by countless small marshes, making one wonder if there isn't more water than land in the vicinity. The nation's mixture of grain fields and marshlands has proven its

White-faced whistling duck.

screamer, sails low over our blind, casting a foreboding shadow. The *chaja* is a prehistoric-looking bird that glides in a manner one might expect from a pterodactyl left over in this land that time has seemingly forgotten.

Farther down the shallow marsh, Californians Bob Nichols and Leland Scheu are busily testing their shooting skills on a flight of silver teal. Across the marsh, hidden in a blind of reeds, Sam and Sue Campbell, a Tennessee couple, are alternat-

south all the way to Argentina. Silver teal, a duck larger than any of the North American teal, is also abundant and as challenging to hit as its brethren the world over. The brown pintail, though not common here, is present and resembles our northern pintail with a coating of mocha. There are others, too, and a morning in an Argentinean duck blind gives one ample opportunity to learn to identify them on the wing by the color, wingbeat, silhouette, and sound of their calls.

Mellish is my coach for the hunt, whispering the names of the birds as they approach our 50 rosybill decoys—plastic blocks shaped like mallards but painted black and red to match the ever-present rosybills. There is no need for haste when shooting here—a waterfowler will likely never encounter such concentrations of ducks anywhere on the planet. "It's the best duck hunting in the world," says Mellish, a hunter who's searched from Russia to Africa to find the world's finest waterfowling.

As the morning progresses—with Mellish and me taking turns shooting at incoming flights—our host, Pablo Pereira, wanders over to inquire about our success. He's a Uruguayan cattle rancher and part-time polo player who, along with his wife, Pilar, enjoys introducing foreign sportsmen to Argentina's wealth of wildfowl. As we share our hits and misses, an enormous *chaja*, or southern

Above: Patria Chica is just one of several comfortable estancias used by Frontiers. The key is finding such accommodations near the region's best gunning.

Left: A Frontiers shooting party returning to Patria Chica, a half-century-old estancia where they enjoy a delectable brunch— including grilled rosybills over toast.

ability to produce staggering masses of ducks. Hunting pressure in the country is virtually nonexistent, save for a few foreign water-fowlers whose migrations take them to these fabled hunting grounds. Guns and ammunition are both difficult to find and expensive for Argentineans, whose modest incomes seldom allow for such luxuries.

The imported Winchester shells cycle well through my autoloaders. While pumps and double guns often find their way into Argentinean duck blinds, autoloaders are the most commonly used guns for both duck and dove hunting. Since you won't readily find

ty and reliability over the years. We stand thigh-deep in water, surrounded by a rectangle of thin tree branches temporarily stuck into the clay bottom of the marsh. As light illuminates the grayness of the low fog that cloaks the marsh, flights of ducks—ranging from 10 to 30 in a flock—stream toward our decoys. The descending masses look like approaching jets at a busy airport, one behind the other as far as the eye is able to penetrate the murk.

Actor Jameson Parker returns with a load of rosybills to a stunning Argentinean estancia operated by Frontiers.

Above right: Jameson Parker unearths a perdiz with the help of a pointer. Note the extremely short tail on the bird. This accounts for the birds' erratic flight patterns.

gunsmiths on the pampas, it's a good idea to bring along two guns and spare gun parts on any South American wingshooting foray. Be sure guns are in good working order before the trip because new heights of frustration are often reached when having to sacrifice hunting time for the lack of working armament.

To reduce the chances of gun problems, both Mellish and I use Beretta A303s, repeaters that have proven both their durabili-

Above: A pointer rests before embarking on an afternoon perdiz hunt. Perdiz, or spotted tinamou, are not partridge at all, but rather are in the rhea family.

Left: Sometimes the ducks don't so much flock in Argentina as they swarm. Here thousands of rosybills cover an expansive marsh.

The first in are the silver teal, strafing the blocks from cattail height, here and gone before guns can greet them. Soon a great concentration of rosy-billed pochards, whistling ducks, and Brazilian ducks are massing overhead, all in what seems an effort to reach our decoys. It is at that moment that I understand why Mellish and others have become something akin to seasonal residents of the pampas.

The hunter's high, borne of the euphoria of so many birds at such close proximity, is nothing short of addictive, and to find it with regularity you must go to Argentina, where ducks still darken the sky like the birds in dreams.

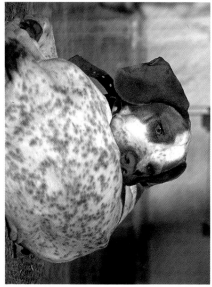

Picazuro pigeon (Columba picazuro).

CHAPTER 15

Alberto's Time
⌒ URUGUAY ⌒

I am not one for generalizations, but I've encountered Italians in hunting camps from Africa to Europe to South America, and no matter how far they travel from their motherland, they carry with them a zest for life unlike that of any other people on the planet. They celebrate their every breath as though tomorrow is merely a hope. Share a hunting lodge with one and it's doubtful that you'll ever be the same.

Though his address says Montevideo, Uruguay, Alberto Regusci's roots are as Italian as rigatoni. The boisterous Italian-cum-Uruguayan is never far from excitement; he orchestrates wingshooting safaris throughout the mostly agrarian country of Uruguay. This small nation of some 3 million inhabitants lies just north of Argentina and is increasingly becoming the destination of choice for foreign wingshooters who previously only traveled to Argentina or Colombia. Expansive grain fields, including sorghum, stretch across the open plain west of the capital of Montevideo. Millet means doves—swarms of the birds. Several species of pigeon also cloud the region, including the robust spot-winged and picazuro varieties.

A group of American sports revel in what is the world's finest dove shooting. They have come to Uruguay to shoot doves, and they will return home with sore shoulders.

Above: Alberto Regusci lives it up with one of the kitchen help at an estancia in Uruguay. In addition to being one of the finest wingshots I have ever seen, Regusci is always the life of the party.

Right: The Uruguayan combo: a tinamou (upper left) is flanked by a pair of spot-wing pigeons and the teal-sized picazuro pigeon.

Opposite page: There is an undeniable European influence in Uruguay that extends all the way to the bird shooting as experienced by these gunners in full costume. (Photo by R. Valentine Atkinson.)

THE WORLD'S GREATEST WINGSHOOTING DESTINATIONS

144

With sometimes lengthy drives, Regusci revels in the art of conversation, putting miles behind us with every anecdote. He begins stories as a way to engage his passengers, knowing that what people most want to hear is their own voices. With the discussion well primed, Regusci surrenders the rest of the dialogue to Bob Nichols and Leland Scheu, a pair of fiftysomething Californians, and to Covell Brown, an American businessman now living in Canada. I, like Regusci, mostly look and listen.

Our destination is La Esperanza near the community of Trinidad, one of nine *estancias* Regusci uses to house his sports for gunning forays, lodging near the shooting fields that Regusci locates personally. "I know what foreign hunters want," he says, "so I inspect the bird fields myself." He works in concert with Luis Brown, a U.S.-educated Uruguayan who received his MBA at the Wharton School of Business. While Regusci coordinates the dove, pigeon, and perdiz shooting, Brown specializes in duck hunting in both Argentina and Uruguay, forming the long-running, highly successful River Platte Wingshooting Adventures.

The countryside reminds one of parts of Kansas: tempered climbs and gentle descents and only sparse tree cover. Small groves of eucalyptus—enough to roost the region's population of doves—dot the otherwise open land-

scape. We pass fields with *nandu,* ostrich-like birds that stare stupidly at our vehicle. Cattle graze in many fields since the Uruguayans, like their Argentinean counterparts, savor an abundance of beef in their diets.

Doves and pigeons crisscross the air as we arrive at the *estancia,* but the area's perdiz, a gringo colloquialism that is commonly used to describe a variety of partridge-like birds, will be the center of our focus at the outset of our journey. The perdiz are sporting birds with robust flushes and are especially shy when pointing dogs crowd them. For Carlos Corellezze and his young Brittany, Tuqui, the perdiz present ever-challenging prospects as the guide and his dog lead gunners to the birds.

Covell Brown joins me as we course a grazed field, walking at port arms as Corellezze and the Brittany comb the field ahead of us in search of the birds. There seems nary enough cover to conceal a shrew, but I follow the Brittany on faith—a lesson learned from years of following good bird dogs. Tuqui is a classic French Brittany with a small frame and pointed muzzle—far different from so many of the big-running, Stateside Brittanys that resemble English setters with docked tails.

The dog's demeanor changes the instant it encounters the scent of a perdiz. Its steady gallop becomes an almost spastic darting until the pointing instinct takes control and the dog

peers intently at a foot-tall tuft of grass still 20 yards ahead. Brown and I flank the dog, walking gingerly ahead to flush the bird—repeating the butt-belly-beak-bang sequence in my mind as I stride forward. Perhaps five steps past the pup, the perdiz flushes in a flurry of pinions, quartering ahead of Brown in low trajectory. Brown misses with his first shot but sends the tinamou to the plains with the load from his second barrel. We encounter another 20 birds in our morning walk, most sitting at the end of points. The birds' knack for flushing 15 to 20 yards ahead of the dog is reminiscent of the skittish nature of ruffed grouse. A rapid gun mount and instinctive shot prove to be the best course for grounding the birds.

Upon finishing the morning hike, Regusci arranges to take us to an *asado,* or South American barbecue. Various cuts of beef and chicken are sizzling on an open grill as we enter the driveway of a nearby farm, eucalyptus trees lining its course like living pillars. Uruguayans consume more meat per capita than people in any other country, so it is with sharpened incisors that I look forward to sampling the two-pound steaks. Carlos and his son Rudolpho help tend the fire as the rest of us sip vino and salivate in anticipation of the feast. Regusci helps the farmer's wife place trays of food and exquisite pastries on tables on the stone patio. The two converse in Spanish, and

soon there is infectious laughter throughout the household—an occurrence that seems to follow Regusci wherever he goes. After the *asado*, we sip *mate*, a drink derived from dried herbs that has no caffeine but possesses twice the uplifting effect. The crushed herb leaves look like the dried parsley college junkies sometimes tried to peddle as cannabis. Whatever the contents, Regusci, Scheu, Nichols, and Brown begin taking turns dancing with the farmer's wife. It reminds me of the ballroom scene in the film *Cocoon*, where the geriatrics, now invigorated by their swims in rejuvenating alien waters, temporarily forget about their osteoporosis and artificial hips and boogie till the break of dawn. I stand back and record the scene on film—the kind of blackmail material that accounts for the real way a writer/photographer earns *dinero*.

PIGEON ENGLISH

When heading to a Uruguayan dove and pigeon field, a gringo should know at least one Spanish phrase: *"Por favor, mas cartuches"* (More cartridges, please)! Though it is not even considered the prime season for doves and pigeons, a staggering aggregation of the birds infest the

It's not uncommon to enjoy 40 or 50 tinamou flushes a day in a good Uruguayan perdiz field— if you have access to an experienced dog.

400-acre sorghum field that lies before us. They lift en masse only to flutter back to the field, presumably testing themselves to see if they're yet too engorged to fly. To local farmers, the birds resemble a plague of biblical proportions. The flocks resemble giant pods of krill forced to the surface by marauding whales.

Call me Ishmael. Soon the doves and pigeons are confused by my shooting, flying

in a chaotic scramble to find a quiet corner of the grain in which they can resume their feasting. The other shooters begin firing up and down the field, and from the distance, the birds appear like locusts over an Egyptian cotton field.

I pause long enough to watch Regusci pluck a trio of ridiculously high doves from the sky. I would have thought such fortune was

mere luck, but he continues his prowess—passing on easy shots for the high sailers. Regusci is living proof that an unlimited supply of birds and an equal amount of cartridges are important ingredients when producing an exceptional wingshot. Perhaps it is these two factors—more than his Italian ancestry—that explain his consistent good cheer and eternal thirst for the hunt. Perhaps.

CHAPTER 16

Andean Magic
~ ECUADOR ~

ne glance through the picture window and I know I'm a long way from home—perhaps 100 years. Across a vast canyon rests a series of huts. Outside the shacks, farmers draped in brilliant alpaca weaves hoe the land much the way their ancestors have since the Incan Empire spanned a good portion of South America. Behind the laborers broods a dramatic peak—towering ominously above reason. Its pinnacle appears like an immense snow cone cloaked by pillowy clouds. The cumulus formations bleed a violet hue as the sun emerges behind them.

Yesterday I stood on the 45th parallel; today I'm straddling the equator. I left a drizzly southern Wisconsin, flew to Miami, passed Cuba, and landed in Quito, Ecuador, a mountain oasis resting at twice the elevation of Denver. I did this in the time that it would have taken neolithic man to fashion a crude ax-head from stone. Indeed, the modern age isn't without virtue.

Quito rises above an ocean of jungle, leaving mosquitoes and malaria behind in the humid solarium of the forest lowlands. At such elevation, the city skyline tickles the belly of passing clouds, leaving one to wonder if early visitors climbed beanstalks to access the region.

A mixed pot of doves and perdiz that were transformed into grilled delicacies upon our return to Quito.

My brother (left) and Jim Anders climb the high-mountain wheat fields above Quito, Ecuador, in search of tinamou.
Anders' dog, a Texas-born Brittany, proved skillful in finding the perdiz hidden among the grain.

THE WORLE'S GREATEST WINGSHOOTING DESTINATIONS

150

As much as this city has to offer—with its Spanish architecture, clean streets, and bustling markets—my stay is going to be abbreviated. In the living room, my brother stuffs duffel bags with box upon box of Winchester AA 20-gauge cartridges, enough to mount a limited military campaign.

"Think you're being a little overly optimistic, Joe?" I query as he continues piling the field loads into the burgeoning bag.

"I ran out last time I went up," he says. "I'll be damned if that's going to happen again."

I had heard the reports of a nearly endless stream of doves pouring from the eucalyptus groves that dot the Ecuadoran mountain slopes, but there is a fine line between optimism and overconfidence. Though an Australian import, eucalyptus trees grow exceedingly well across much of South America and have been adopted by the doves as a favorite nesting and roosting habitat. The soft fiber of the fast-growing tree is used to manufacture diapers Stateside. The thought of razing a tree that once fortified the slopes of the Andes, however, to cover a leaky bottom doesn't seem altogether noble—at least not in the same way a walnut is cut to become the palette upon which a fine gun maker works his artistic magic.

Joining us on the ascent to the bird fields is Jim Anders, another American import who, like my brother, is on diplomatic assignment

We are hunting at perhaps three times the elevation of Denver, so I use the camera as my excuse to get my partners to pause so that I can take this photo of the dramatic Andeanscape.

with the American Embassy in Quito. I sit in the back seat of Anders' Blazer as we embark on the three-hour drive to the sweeping wheat fields where, we hope, there will be doves. Even the steep slopes of the Andean peaks are cultivated in a crude patchwork of grain in varying stages of growth. The look is one of an expansive quilt draped over the landscape. Erosion control is a concept as foreign to the nation's farmers as space travel, as even steep grades are cultivated—usually in rows running with the grade of the slope.

The farther we journey from Quito, the more difficult our passage becomes, an axiom true almost anywhere in the developing world. The concrete pavement gives way to gravel, which surrenders to little more than a wagon trail. We twist our way amid frightening gorges, polished by rivers that snake through the landscape—often spilling into waterfalls arched by mist rainbows. We inch across several small bridges, and soon it is clear that the journey to the shoot becomes the real adventure of the expedition.

Our meanderings through the Ecuadoran countryside, however, bring us to a small village that looks incarnated from a Discovery Channel documentary. Peasant farmers hoe the sandy loam around a plot of maize while a trio of small children run in and out of an adobe hut. In a small enclosure, a black pig of gargantuan proportions roots in the mud, its long, wooly hair making it appear more a member of the ursine clan than the porcine family. Raking the dirt next to the pig are a dozen chickens that look as though they're bustard hybrids. Their outlandishly long legs and raptorlike heads lead one to believe they probably don't surrender their eggs without a great deal of finesse by the peasants.

Above: South American dove shooting is unmatched anywhere in the world. Find a freshly harvested grain field next to a large roost and you had better have brought plenty of shells.

Opposite page: Only a lack of daylight could keep us from our appointment with the doves. We face a three-hour drive back to Quito down dicey mountain roads before we reach home.

Two canyons beyond the village and we enter what seems another climate, an ecotone unto itself as if enclosed in some sort of a cosmic-sized terrarium. We leave the semiarid eastern slope and are now facing the morning sun. The mountain peaks make storm clouds pay toll in the form of rain before passing overhead. The slopes here are lush with succulent growth. There are no discernable seasons on the equator, so the land is worked tirelessly—albeit in an almost feudal fashion—in an attempt to feed the ever-expanding human population.

Some of that grain, however, fattens the region's other inhabitants: doves and perdiz. The doves appear indistinguishable from our own mourning dove, while the tinamou is a grassland dweller roughly the dimensions of a Hungarian partridge. The birds are seldom found in coveys, and Anders' Texas-born Brittany weaves his way through wheat fields in a ceaseless quest for them. Overhead, an endless current of doves passes by, reminding me of the seasonal blackbird migrations Stateside.

The abundance of birds waiting within reach of our trigger fingers has a strange calming effect. There is no urgency to shoot because there is no sense that opportunities will be limited. The wind in our ears deafens us, suspending conversation and focusing our attention to the sky in a spellbinding, almost surreal moment. I feel suspended in time, as if I'm witnessing the last of the great passenger pigeon flights. I wonder if my ancestors ever shared such hypnosis before the pigeons went the way of the dodo.

We divert from the tinamou walk because the gusty wind plays havoc with the Brittany's ability to decipher scent. The endless climb of the slopes is a radical departure from the aspen woods of the Great Lakes, where I developed what little shooting technique to which I can lay claim. I sit below the rim of a canyon, just

out of a smashing blow of wind that squeezes through a narrow pass created by a brace of volcanic peaks. The avalanche of doves cascading off the mountain with the torque of the wind behind them renders the shooting futile. My gun seems made of lead, as every feeble shot sails ridiculously behind its target—like a nightmare where you can't reach an object forever just beyond your grasp.

The birds twist and dive in wicked gyrations that suggest their feathers might be sucked from their hides in the vacuum of the whirlwind. I ponder whether the doves will be able to slow their rapid descent before catapulting into the eucalyptus groves below. The guts of nearly a full box of shells pass through my 20 before a single dove falls. I estimate the lead to be 25 feet. Three more birds fall in a dozen subsequent attempts. For the first time, I wonder if Joe packed an adequate number of shells. At such a success rate, we'll return with enough birds to feed a family—of rodents. Each successful shot has more to do with prayer than it does synchronized eye-to-hand coordination.

The wind fades as the sun begins to set. Anders shaves thin strips of cheddar with his pocketknife as we return to the vehicle to collect our memories. We mix the flavor of cheese and apple in our palates, watching silently as time stands still in the Third World.

Spotted tinamou (Nothura maculosa).

CHAPTER 17

The Pisco Shuffle
⌐ PERU ⌐

A dd three jiggers Pisco to one jigger simple syrup and mix with one jigger lemon juice and one egg white and shake with cracked ice and a dash of Angostura bitters and you have the ingredients for the Peruvian national drink—the Pisco sour. The concoction also doubles as a recipe for a hangover. Its effects hit me like a fist to the abdomen the morning after an evening of merriment. Every bump and turn in the road leading to the Andean bird fields taps my cranium like a spastic woodpecker lodged inside my temple. The rugged peaks are the lairs of the spotted tinamou, or *perdiz* as they are more commonly called. I've known dry streambeds to be smoother than the trail upon which we're now driving. Groans, squeaks, and tremors emanate from the Suburban . . . the vehicle protests as well.

I share the ride with brother Joe and nephew Kevin—fellow sufferers on the hemorrhoid trail. We're ascending the mountains surrounding the city of Lima, a forgettable metropolis on South America's mustn't-see tour. If it weren't for crime, filth, and poverty, the city would have few distinguishing characteristics. To

Shortly after snapping this photo of a Peruvian villager and her daughter, the woman held out a cup while saying, "Change please." Capitalism has, indeed, arrived in Peru.

Above and left: A small Munsterlander—a European pointing breed similar in size to an English setter—retrieves a tinamou taken by my brother. The Munsterlander is an extremely biddable breed that makes quick work of tinamou. (Photos by Joe Dorsey.)

Opposite page: No wingshooter traveler to Peru should miss the chance to visit the spectacular Incan ruins of Machu Picchu located high in the Andes.

top if off, it virtually never rains in Lima, so the metropolis forever looks as though it needs to wash its face. By virtue of wise planning, my stay in Lima is mercifully short. Our destination, instead, is the high steppes inhabited only by sheep and goat herders, a lonely land where the air is thin and your feet are heavy. From the mountaintops, the choked streets and chaotic mayhem of Lima seem centuries removed.

As we uncase our guns, I survey what appears little more than a bald pasture with rows of rock-pile fences reminiscent of the Irish countryside, sans water. Although I don't perceive an absence of oxygen at first, a lightheaded sensation and lack of stamina settle over me—the same sort of malaise that sets in when it's time to paint the house or rake the yard. I say nothing, fearing it's the second stage of Pisco poisoning and not the altitude at all.

"Take it easy up here," advises Joe. "You feel like you're on the moon in this air."

I find myself moving in slow motion, strangely uncoordinated—as if walking

Right: A cure for hardmouth? The position of this fallen tinamou made for a delicate retrieve.

Opposite page. The edges surrounding cultivated fields provide ideal places to find tinamou. The birds use the cover to hide and loaf throughout most of the day before returning to feed in the fields each morning and evening. (Photos by Joe Dorsey.)

Winding down after a day of stalking perdiz at 13,000 feet, my sea-level legs and lungs were ready for a rest. Peru sits in the midst of the continental spine that is the Andes Mountains, one of the world's tallest chains.

against the current of a stream. My brother's small Munsterlander bumps a perdiz, the bird corkscrewing in flight as Joe shoots and tumbles it. The scene seems surreal in my altered state, like I've been thrust into some sort of avant-garde film. I've hunted perdiz from Argentina and Uruguay to Ecuador and now Peru. They vary in size from almost quail proportions to ruffed grouse dimensions—their toffee plumage concealing them even in whisker-length cover. While exploring South America, the Spanish conquistadors encountered the birds and likened them to their native partridge (red-legs). Hence, they used the Latin name for partridge (*perdix*), from which the common moniker of perdiz was derived.

We fan out across this highland pasture, looking down on a sea of clouds that gives the illusion that we're traversing an island. Joe keeps an eye on Kevin, whose slouched posture hints that he's feeling the effects of the altitude, but much like his father at 13, Kevin will let little stand in the way of a chance to hunt.

The pointer makes game again, picking its way through and around a loose pile of football-sized rocks. With such sparse cover, the birds have little interest in holding long enough for the dog to point them. A bird flushes 15 yards ahead on the other side of a rock wall. It quarters away, heading downs-lope yet rising from the ground. The illusion is that the bird is climbing above me when, in fact, it is not. It is a revelation that seizes me the moment I finish missing the second of two shots. It's like the one shot on a sporting clays course that no one can seem to make—except for the local ringer who's shot the station so often that he's committed every angle to mem-ory. You'll know him because he'll be the one grinning like a Cheshire cat while watching everyone else miss.

To my left, near a precipice that seemingly drops into the clouds, Joe snatches a distant bird as it is about to vanish into the pillowy abyss. Before that bird bounces to the rocks, another flushes, suffering the same fate as its predecessor. There's meat for the pot—and a succulent white meat it is.

We pause to collect the birds . . . and our breath. Some 300 yards upslope, a herdsman brings a small band of goats across the field as though making his morning commute. It is a scene straight from the pages of *National Geographic*. We continue on our sweep of the mountainside, sans goats. Despite my deadened shooting reflexes, I eventually overtake a bird and send it tumbling in an instant, the image freeze-framed in my mind's eye. It's a memory that serves me well: I recall the lead as I snuff the next three perdiz as though shooting trap from the 16-yard line. The best shooters have good memories—as fortune would have it, mine is only average.

A return to the Suburban gives us a chance to quench our thirsts and our appetites. The effects of the Pisco sours begin to oxidize from my pores. Now it is only the altitude that grips me like an anaconda around my chest. The pointer chokes for air as well, panting heavily as it rests under the shade of the tailgate. Young dogs—like young people—often lack pace, a truth apparent in the budding pointer. In my world of travels with gun dogs, only a handful of those canines had the good sense to measure their tempo, and in each case the dogs were more than 5 years old. It remains one of the most valuable traits of a truly great bird dog, and it's not a characteristic that can be taught.

After our respite, we continue our proces-sion across the mountainside. The stone-lined fields look faintly reminiscent of Machu Picchu, the famed Inca ruins farther east in the Andean range. The ancient city perched in the clouds of the Peruvian jungles is the most spectacular of the lost civilizations, a fortress of stone crown-ing a mountain spire. Visiting Peru without seeing Machu Picchu is like touring Egypt without setting sight on the pyramids. As mountains go, the Andes are among the tallest chain in the world. The highest peak in the Peruvian Andes is Mt. Huascaran, a dormant volcano that stands 22,205 feet above sea level.

Fatigue plays more of a factor in determin-ing the length of a mountain wingshooting foray than does the abundance of birds. Having made a successful exploratory mission, Joe makes plans to return with tents and gas stoves for an extended perdiz visitation. Save for the bumps along the trail, I'll remember fondly my journey to the highlands. Though I might be 5,000 miles away, I will make the next pilgrim-age to the peaks with my brother in spirit, if not in person.